MINI

ENCYCLOPEDIA

SPACE

D1113883

ENCYCLOPEDIA

SPACE

Miles
Kelly

First published as Space in 2009 by Miles Kelly Publishing Ltd
Harding's Barn, Bardfield End Green, Thaxted, Essex, CM6 3PX, UK

Copyright © Miles Kelly Publishing Ltd 2009

This edition published in 2014

2 4 6 8 10 9 7 5 3

Publishing Director Belinda Gallagher
Creative Director Jo Cowan
Series Designer Helen Bracey
Volume Designer Rocket Design Ltd
Cover Designer Jo Cowan
Indexer Eleanor Holme
Production Manager Elizabeth Collins
Reprographics Stephan Davis, Jennifer Cozens, Anthony Cambray
Assets Lorraine King
Contributors Sue Becklake, John Farndon,
Tim Furniss, Clint Twist

ISBN 978-1-78209-449-4

Printed in China

British Library Cataloguing-in-Publication Data
A catalogue record for this book is available from the British Library

Made with paper from a sustainable forest

www.mileskelly.net
info@mileskelly.net

Contents

Exploring space

Astronomy

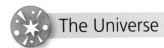

The Universe

Stars and galaxies

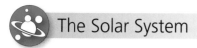

The Solar System

Constellations

Exploring space

Space

- **There is no internationally accepted definition** of where space begins. The International Aeronautical Federation (FAI) recognizes the Karman line 100 km above the Earth's surface as being the boundary between the atmosphere and space.

- **The region around our Solar System** is known as local space. The space between the stars in our galaxy is known as interstellar space, and beyond that is intergalactic space.

- **Contrary to popular belief**, space is not an empty vacuum – it is a near vacuum. Each cubic kilometre contains a few drifting atoms of gas and dust.

- **In the region of the Sun**, this interstellar medium consists of about 90 percent hydrogen, 9 percent helium and one percent dust.

- **The interstellar dust** consists of tiny grains composed mainly of silicate (silicon and oxygen) and graphite (carbon), as well as small amounts of iron.

- **Between galaxies**, the intergalactic medium consists mostly of ionized hydrogen – atoms of hydrogen gas that have had their electron stripped away.

- **Space is so big** that miles and kilometres become meaningless, which is why people often use the word 'astronomical' to describe exceptionally large numbers.

- **In local space**, distances are often measured in AUs (Astronomical Units) – one AU is 147,000,000 km (the average distance between the Earth and the Sun).

● **Interstellar space** is usually measured in light years (ly). One light year is about 9.5 trillion km (the distance light travels in one year).

● **Some astronomers prefer** to measure large distances in parsecs (pc). One parsec equals 3.26 light years, and a kiloparsec (kpc) is 1000 parsecs and a megaparsec (mpc) is 1,000,000 parsecs.

▼ *The Andromeda Galaxy (M31), the nearest spiral galaxy to our own, viewed across 740 kiloparsecs (about 2.4 million light years) of intergalactic space.*

Space travel

🪐 **In 1957**, the first artificial satellite, the Soviet *Sputnik 1*, was launched into space.

🪐 **A dog, Laika**, was the first living creature in space on *Sputnik 2* in 1957. Laika died when the spacecraft's oxygen supply ran out.

🪐 **The first manned space flight** was made in April 1961 by the Soviet cosmonaut Yuri Gagarin in *Vostok 1*.

🪐 **In February 1966**, the first controlled Moon landing was made by the Soviet *Luna 9*.

🪐 **In 1970**, the Soviet *Venera 7* was the first probe to touch down on another planet.

🪐 **Unmanned space probes** have visited all the planets and flown to the edge of the Solar System.

🪐 **The arrival of the space shuttle** in 1981 made working in orbit much easier.

🪐 **Cosmonaut Valeri Poliakov** spent 437 days on board the *Mir* space station.

🪐 **Astronauts have lived** on the International Space Station since 2001, staying for six months at a time.

◀ *Laika, the first living creature in space, travelled in the Soviet spacecraft,* Sputnik 2.

DID YOU KNOW?

In 2003, China became the third nation to launch an astronaut into orbit.

▲ Russia's Mir space station, connected to Atlantis space shuttle. Mir was launched in 1986 and made 76,000 orbits of Earth before it was crashed into the Pacific Ocean in 2001.

Space exploration

- **Space is explored in two ways** – by studying it from Earth using powerful telescopes, and by launching spacecraft to get a closer view.

- **Most space exploration** is by unmanned space probes.

- **The first pictures** of the far side of the Moon were sent back by the *Luna 3* space probe in October 1959.

- **Manned missions have only reached** as far as the Moon and no one has been back there since 1972.

- **Apollo astronauts took** three days to reach the Moon.

- **A journey to the stars** would take hundreds of years. One idea is that humans could travel there inside gigantic spaceships made from hollowed-out asteroids.

- **Another idea is that spacecraft** on long voyages of exploration may be driven along by nuclear power.

- **The *Pioneer* and *Voyager* probes** carry information about life on Earth in case they are found by extraterrestrial life.

- **A probe has never** come back from another planet.

DID YOU KNOW?
NASA plans to send astronauts back to the Moon by 2020, followed by manned missions to Mars.

▲ The first successful planetary probe was the USA's Mariner 2, which flew past Venus in 1962.

Spacecraft

🪐 **There are three kinds of spacecraft** – artificial satellites, unmanned probes and manned spacecraft.

🪐 **Spacecraft have double hulls** (outer coverings) for protection against other space objects that crash into them.

🪐 **Manned spacecraft must also provide** air pressure to prevent the crew's blood from boiling.

🪐 **Spacecraft windows have filters** to shield astronauts from the Sun's dangerous ultraviolet rays.

🪐 **Radiators on the outside** of the spacecraft lose excess heat from electrical equipment and the crew's bodies.

🪐 **Manned spacecraft** have life-support systems that provide oxygen to breathe, usually mixed with nitrogen (as in ordinary air).

🪐 **The carbon dioxide** that the crew breathes out is absorbed by zeolite or lithium hydroxide.

> **DID YOU KNOW?**
> Astronauts would float when asleep if they were not strapped down in a sleeping bag.

🪐 **Astronauts use a waterproof shower** that sprays water from all sides and then removes the waste water.

🪐 **Spacecraft toilets** need to get rid of waste in low gravity conditions. Astronauts have to sit on a device that sucks away the waste. Solid waste is dried and returned to Earth.

▲ *The US space shuttle, the first reusable spacecraft, has made regular manned space flights into orbit and back to Earth.*

Astronauts

🪐 **The first astronauts** were jet pilots.

🪐 **In the USA** an astronaut is defined as anyone who has flown at an altitude of more than 80 km above sea level, which includes some aircraft test pilots.

DID YOU KNOW?
Weightlessness makes astronauts grow several centimetres during a long mission.

🪐 **The US space shuttle carries** three kinds of astronaut – pilots, mission specialists and payload specialists.

🪐 **A pilot or commander's job** is to be responsible for the mission and to control the spacecraft.

🪐 **Mission specialists** are crew members who carry out specific jobs, such as running experiments or going on space walks.

🪐 **Payload specialists** are not NASA astronauts, but scientists and other onboard guests.

🪐 **Astronauts on long missions** use exercise machines to keep fit.

🪐 **The first woman in space** was cosmonaut Valentina Tereshkova, who completed 48 orbits of the Earth in June 1963.

🪐 **The first 'space-tourist'** was American Dennis Tito who is reported to have paid $20 million to spend nearly eight days aboard a Russian Soyuz spacecraft in 2001. Several other people have subsequently 'paid their own ticket' to get into space.

▼ Astronauts train for months to deal with the demands of space missions. They learn to fly the shuttle in simulators and training aircraft.

Astronaut training

🪐 **A bachelor's degree** in science, maths or engineering and a minimum of three years professional experience are the basic qualifications for astronaut training.

🪐 **The American space agency, NASA,** trains astronauts at the Johnson Space Center near Houston, Texas. The training lasts between 12 and 22 months.

▼ *The buoyancy provided by water in a training pool allows space-suited astronauts to become familiar with the techniques of manoeuvring in weightless conditions.*

- **At NASA**, a silver lapel pin is given to people who successfully complete the astronaut training program. Once they have flown in space, they receive a gold pin.

- **Visitors to the Kennedy Space Center**, near Orlando, Florida, can sign up for between one to three days of astronaut training.

- **Early astronauts** were familiarized with the extreme forces experienced during lift-off by being fired along a rail aboard a rocket-powered sled at speeds of up to 900 km/h.

- **Huge spinning centrifuges** are now used to ensure that potential astronauts can withstand the strong 'G-forces' that can be expected during a flight into space.

- **Astronauts practise** for space walks in a huge tank of water that simulates weightlessness through neutral buoyancy.

- **The Neutral Buoyancy Research Facility** at the University of Maryland is used to develop new techniques for EVAs and the use of robots in space.

- **During training**, astronauts experience short periods of actual weightlessness aboard a plunging jet aircraft. They are also exposed to very high and very low atmospheric pressure.

- **Astronauts train** to use the latest MMU backpacks using a virtual reality simulator that is said to be almost as 'real' as the real thing.

- **The C11-A shuttle training aircraft**, which has the same atmospheric handling qualities as the space shuttle, is based at Ellington Field, close to the Johnson Space Center.

Take-off

3 Main fuel tank falls away 130 km up – this is the second stage

2 Solid-fuel rocket burners fall away 45 km up – this is the first stage

1 Shuttle blasts off using its engines and two solid rocket boosters

▲ *Powerful rockets are needed to boost a spacecraft to the speed it needs to overcome the Earth's gravity.*

- **When a spacecraft is launched**, it needs to overcome the pull of the Earth's gravity.

- **In order to escape Earth's gravity**, a spacecraft must be launched at a particular velocity (speed and direction).

- **The minimum velocity needed** for a spacecraft to combat gravity and stay in orbit around the Earth is called the orbital velocity.

- **When a spacecraft reaches** 140 percent of the orbital velocity, it can break free of Earth's gravity. This is called the escape velocity.

- **The thrust (push) that launches** a spacecraft comes from powerful rockets called launch vehicles.

- **Launch vehicles are divided** into sections called stages, which fall away as their task is done.

- **The first stage lifts everything** off the ground, so its thrust must be greater than the weight of the launch vehicle plus the spacecraft. It falls away a few minutes after take off.

- **A second stage is then needed** to accelerate the spacecraft towards space.

- **After the two launch stages fall away**, a third stage puts the spacecraft into orbit.

- **To stay in orbit 200 km above Earth**, a spacecraft flies at more than 8 km/sec.

Rockets

🪐 **The huge thrust needed** to overcome the pull of Earth's gravity and launch a spacecraft into space is provided by rockets.

🪐 **Hot gases that drive the rocket** upwards are produced when rockets burn propellant.

🪐 **Rocket propellant comes in two parts** – a fuel and an oxidizer, which allows the fuel to burn.

🪐 **In solid fuel**, the fuel and oxidizer are chemicals mixed together to make a rubbery substance.

🪐 **Liquid fuel is sometimes liquid hydrogen**, and it is typically used in big rockets.

🪐 **There is no oxygen in space** and the oxidizer supplies the oxygen needed to burn fuel. It is often liquid oxygen (called 'lox' for short).

🪐 **The first rockets** were made 1000 years ago in China.

🪐 **The German V2 war rocket**, designed by Werner von Braun, was the first rocket capable of reaching space.

DID YOU KNOW?

The most powerful rocket ever was Saturn 5, which sent astronauts to the Moon.

▼ *Robert Goddard launched the first liquid-fuel rocket in 1926. It stayed in the air for 2.5 seconds and climbed to a height of 12 m.*

Propulsion

- **Rocket motors** are useful for launching vehicles into space, but they are impractical for long distance travel because of the weight of fuel and oxidizer needed to power the motor.

- **An alternative means** of propulsion for space vehicles is the ion drive engine.

- **Ion drive engines** use an electrical field to ionize atoms and accelerate them out of the back of the engine. This stream of ions produces the thrust that drives the spacecraft forwards.

- **An additional advantage** of the ion drive engine is that it can run at full throttle for months without deteriorating.

- **For journeys within the Solar System**, some scientists plan to use spacecraft that will be propelled by harnessing the power of the Sun with a solar sail.

- **The proposed solar sail** would be at least 1000 m across and made of a highly reflective material. The force of sunlight and the solar wind against the sail would push the craft gently away from the Sun.

- **A more controversial idea** is to use nuclear engines to power spacecraft. Some experiments were carried out in the 1960s but were discontinued because of public fears about radiation.

DID YOU KNOW?

In 1999, NASA successfully tested an ion drive engine aboard the space probe Deep Space I.

🪐 **In its crudest form**, a nuclear space engine consists of a series of small atomic bombs exploded against the underside of an immensely strong dish-shaped metal structure.

🪐 **A futuristic idea** for interstellar travel is to use a hydrogen ram-scoop engine that would collect fuel from clouds of interstellar gas as it went along.

▲ *NASA's experimental ion drive engine mounted at the rear of a spacecraft that has been covered with gold foil to protect its delicate instruments from cosmic radiation.*

Satellites

🪐 **Objects that orbit planets** and other space objects are called satellites. Moons are natural satellites. Spacecraft that orbit the Earth are artificial satellites.

🪐 **The first artificial satellite** was *Sputnik 1*, launched on 4 October 1957.

🪐 **Over 50 artificial satellites** are now launched every year. A few of them are space telescopes.

🪐 **Navigation satellites**, such as the Global Positioning System (GPS), are used by people in ships, planes and cars to work out exactly where they are.

🪐 **Satellites are launched** at a particular speed and trajectory (path) to place them in just the right orbit.

▼ *Communications satellites beam everything from TV pictures to telephone calls around the world.*

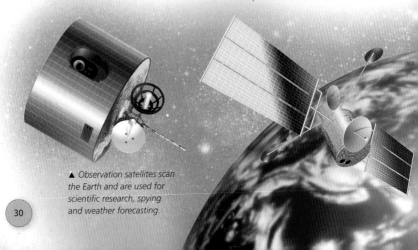

▲ *Observation satellites scan the Earth and are used for scientific research, spying and weather forecasting.*

🪐 **The lower a satellite's orbit,** the faster it must fly to avoid falling back to Earth. Most satellites fly in low orbits less than 1000 km above the Earth.

🪐 **Satellites in geostationary orbit** over the Equator always stay above exactly the same spot on Earth.

🪐 **Polar orbiting satellites** circle the Earth from pole to pole about 850 km up, covering a different strip of the Earth's surface on each orbit.

▲ Satellite telescopes let astronomers look far out into the Universe.

◀ Pictures of the Earth taken by satellites can help make very accurate maps.

Orbits

🐚 **An orbit is the path** of one space object around a larger one, held by the pull of gravity. Moons orbit planets and planets orbit stars.

🐚 **Orbits may be circular**, elliptical (oval) or parabolic (open). The orbits of the planets are elliptical.

🐚 **An orbiting space object** is called a satellite.

🐚 **Stars in the Milky Way** have the longest orbits. They can take up to 200 million years to orbit the galaxy's centre.

🐚 **The force of momentum** keeps a satellite moving through space. The amount of momentum a satellite has depends on its mass and speed.

🐚 **A satellite orbits** at the height where its momentum exactly balances the pull of gravity.

🐚 **If the gravitational pull** is greater than a satellite's momentum, it falls in towards the larger space object.

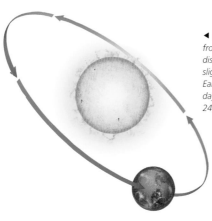

◄ Earth is about 150 million km from the Sun. However, this distance varies as Earth's orbit is slightly oval. The time it takes for Earth to orbit the Sun once is 365 days. In comparison, Pluto takes 248 years to orbit the Sun.

🪐 **If a satellite's momentum** is greater than the pull of gravity, it flies off into space.

🪐 **The lower a satellite orbits**, the faster it must travel to stop it falling in towards the larger space object.

🪐 **Geostationary orbit for one of Earth's artificial satellites** is 35,786 km over the Equator. At this height, it must travel around 11,000 km/h to complete its orbit in 24 hours.

◄ The planets in the Solar System all move round the Sun in elliptical orbits.

33

Space probes

- **Space can be explored using probes** – unmanned, automatic, computer-controlled spacecraft.

- **The first successful planetary probe** was the USA's *Mariner 2*, which flew past Venus in 1962.

- **In 1974**, *Mariner 10* reached Mercury.

- ***Viking 1* and *2* landed** on Mars in 1976.

- ***Voyager 2* has flown** 10 billion km and is heading out of the Solar System after passing close to Jupiter (1979), Saturn (1981), Uranus (1986) and Neptune (1989).

- **Many probes are 'fly-bys'** that spend a few days passing their target and beaming data back to Earth.

- **To save fuel on journeys** to distant planets, space probes may use a nearby planet's gravity to catapult them on their way. This is called a slingshot.

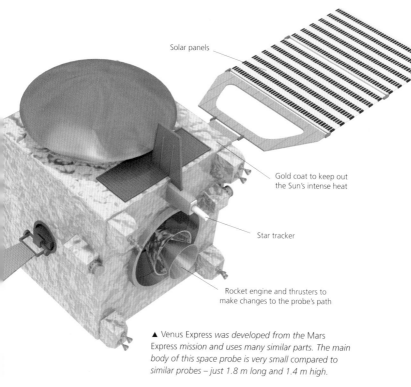

Solar panels

Gold coat to keep out
the Sun's intense heat

Star tracker

Rocket engine and thrusters to
make changes to the probe's path

▲ Venus Express *was developed from the* Mars
Express *mission and uses many similar parts. The main
body of this space probe is very small compared to
similar probes – just 1.8 m long and 1.4 m high.*

🪐 **Probes have orbited** Venus and Mars, mapping their surfaces
   in detail.

🪐 **Rovers have explored** the surface of Mars. Probes have landed on
   Venus, Mars and Saturn's moon, Titan.

🪐 **The *New Horizons* probe** was launched in 2006 and will reach
   Pluto in 2015.

35

Voyagers 1 and 2

◀ Voyager 1 *flew close to Jupiter and Saturn.*

🪐 **The Voyagers are a pair** of unmanned US space probes, launched to explore the outer planets.

🪐 *Voyager 1* **was launched** on 5 September 1977. It flew past Jupiter in March 1979 and Saturn in November 1980, then continued on a curved path to take it out of the Solar System altogether.

🪐 *Voyager 2* **travels** more slowly. Although it was launched two weeks earlier than *Voyager 1*, it did not reach Jupiter until July 1979 and Saturn until August 1981.

🪐 **The Voyagers used** the 'slingshot effect' of Jupiter's gravity to hurl them on towards Saturn.

🪐 **While** *Voyager 1* **headed out** of the Solar System, *Voyager 2* flew past Uranus in January 1986.

Voyager 2 also passed Neptune on 25 August 1989. It took close-up photographs of Uranus and Neptune.

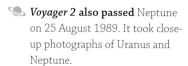

DID YOU KNOW?

Voyager 1 and 2 will beam back data until 2020 as they travel beyond the edges of the Solar System.

▼ Voyager 2 reached Neptune in 1989, revealing a wealth of new information about this distant planet.

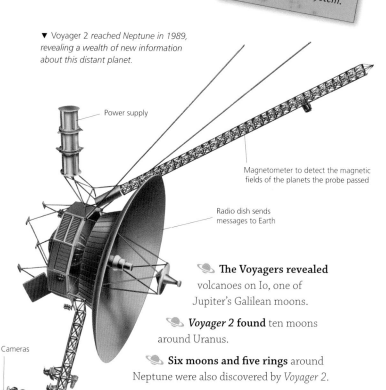

Power supply

Magnetometer to detect the magnetic fields of the planets the probe passed

Radio dish sends messages to Earth

Cameras

The Voyagers revealed volcanoes on Io, one of Jupiter's Galilean moons.

Voyager 2 found ten moons around Uranus.

Six moons and five rings around Neptune were also discovered by _Voyager 2_.

Space shuttle

🪐 **A reusable spacecraft**, the space shuttle is a made up of a 37.2-m-long orbiter, two big Solid Rocket Boosters (SRBs), three main engines and a tank.

🪐 **The shuttle orbiter is launched** into space upright on the SRBs, which fall away to be collected for reuse. When the mission is over, the orbiter lands like a glider.

🪐 **The orbiter can only go as high** as a near-Earth orbit, up to 600 km above the Earth.

🪐 **A basic mission lasts seven days**, and the maximum crew is eight.

🪐 **Orbiter toilets use flowing air** to suck away waste.

🪐 **The crew use** a 'remote manipulator arm' to catch satellites for repair.

🪐 **The shuttle programme** was brought to a temporary halt in 1986 when *Challenger* exploded shortly after launch, killing its crew of seven.

🪐 **On 1 February 2003**, *Columbia* broke up when re-entering the atmosphere after a mission, killing the crew. The next shuttle flight was not until 2006.

▶ *In orbit, the space shuttle circles the Earth at a speed of about 28,000 km/h. Its 18-m-long cargo bay can carry a 25,000-kg load.*

The space shuttle will continue to fly until 2010 in order to finish building the International Space Station.

A replacement for the shuttle is being developed and should be ready to fly in 2014. It is called *Orion* and will be launched on top of a rocket.

▲ The entire centre section of the orbiter is a cargo bay that can be opened in space so satellites can be placed in orbit.

Spacelab, a laboratory where the crew can carry out experiments

Flight deck with pilot's controls

Access tunnel from crew cabin to Spacelab

Crew quarters where astronauts eat, sleep and work

39

Space stations

🪐 **The first space station** was the Soviet *Salyut 1* launched in April 1971. Its low orbit meant it could only stay in space for five months.

🪐 *Skylab* was the first US space station. Three crews spent a total of 171 days there in 1973–74.

🪐 **The longest-serving station** so far was the Soviet *Mir*. Launched in 1986, it made more than 89,000 orbits of the Earth. The last crew left in 2000.

🪐 *Mir* **was built in stages**. It weighed 125 tonnes and had six docking ports, two living rooms, a bathroom and two small individual cabins.

🪐 **There is neither an up nor a down** in a space station, but *Mir* had carpets on the 'floor', pictures on the 'wall' and lights on the 'ceiling'.

🪐 **The giant International Space Station (ISS)** is being built in stages and should be complete in 2011. The first crew boarded the ISS in November 2000.

🪐 **The ISS** will be 108 m in width, 74 m in length and 450 tonnes in weight.

DID YOU KNOW?
The living space on the ISS will be bigger than the passenger space on a 747 jet.

🪐 **When complete, the ISS will have ten sections** where its crew of six astronauts can live and work.

▼ The ISS is made of separate modules fitted together in space.
It is powered by huge solar panels.

Space suits

Camera

🪐 **Astronauts wear space suits** for protection when they go outside their spacecraft. The suits are also called EMUs (Extra-vehicular Mobility Units).

🪐 **The outer layers of a space suit** protect against harmful radiation from the Sun and fast-moving particles of space dust called micrometeoroids.

🪐 **The clear, plastic helmet** also protects against radiation and micrometeoroids.

🪐 **Oxygen is circulated** around the helmet to prevent the visor from misting.

🪐 **The middle layers** of a space suit are blown up like a balloon to press against the astronaut's body. Without this pressure, the astronaut's blood would boil.

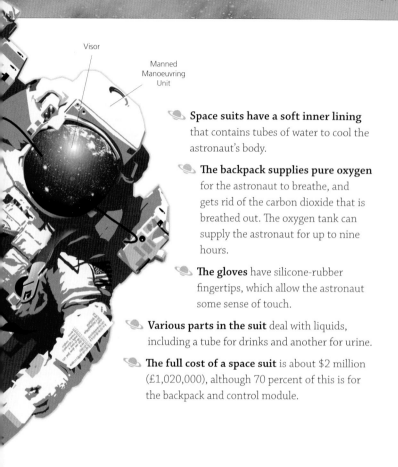

Visor

Manned
Manoeuvring
Unit

🌑 **Space suits have a soft inner lining**
   that contains tubes of water to cool the
   astronaut's body.

🌑 **The backpack supplies pure oxygen**
   for the astronaut to breathe, and
   gets rid of the carbon dioxide that is
   breathed out. The oxygen tank can
   supply the astronaut for up to nine
   hours.

🌑 **The gloves** have silicone-rubber
   fingertips, which allow the astronaut
   some sense of touch.

🌑 **Various parts in the suit** deal with liquids,
   including a tube for drinks and another for urine.

🌑 **The full cost of a space suit** is about $2 million
   (£1,020,000), although 70 percent of this is for
   the backpack and control module.

◀ *Space suits provide a complete life-support system,
including oxygen and water, whilst also protecting
against the dangers of space.*

Space walks

- **The technical name** for going outside a spacecraft is Extra-Vehicular Activity (EVA).

- **In 1965, Soviet cosmonaut, Alexei Leonov**, was the first person to walk in space.

- **During space walks**, a cable called an umbilical keeps the astronauts connected to their spacecraft.

- **A Manned Manoeuvring Unit (MMU)** is a huge rocket-powered backpack that allows astronauts to go further from their spacecraft.

- **In 1984, US astronaut, Bruce McCandless**, was the first person to use an MMU in space.

- **Damages to the *Mir* space station** and other satellites have been repaired by space-walking astronauts.

- **Long space walks** were needed to repair and replace instruments on the Hubble space telescope in the shuttle's payload bay.

- **Russian and US astronauts** use a robotic arm to help them to assemble sections of the International Space Station.

DID YOU KNOW?

Astronauts on space walks may be aided by a flying robot camera the size of a beach ball.

▶ Astronauts wearing MMUs can move away from their spacecraft without fear of floating away.

Moon landings

▼ In 1971, James Irwin stands beside his landing craft with his Moon car, called a Lunar Rover.

- **The first Moon landing** was by the unmanned Soviet *Luna 9* probe, which touched down on the Moon's surface in 1966.

- **In 1961**, the Apollo missions began. Out of the 11 crewed missions, only six managed to land on the Moon.

- **The first men to orbit** the Moon were the astronauts on board the US *Apollo 8* in 1968.

- **On 20 July 1969**, the American astronauts, Edwin 'Buzz' Aldrin and Neil Armstrong, became the first men to walk on the Moon.

- **When Neil Armstrong stepped** onto the Moon for the first time, he said the words, 'That's one small step for a man, one giant leap for mankind'.

- **The Moon astronauts** brought back 380 kg of Moon rock.

- **A mirror was left on** the Moon's surface to reflect a laser beam that measured the Moon's distance from Earth with great accuracy.

- **Lasers can measure the exact distance** to the Moon within an accuracy of 30 cm.

- **Gravity on the Moon** is so weak that astronauts can leap high into the air wearing their heavy space suits.

- **Temperatures typically reach** 105°C at midday on the Moon but plunge to –155°C at night.

Mars landings

🪐 **In the 1970s**, the US *Vikings 1* and *2* and the Soviet *Mars 3* and *5* probes all reached the surface of Mars.

🪐 *Mars 3* **was the first probe** to make a soft landing on Mars on 2 December 1971. It sent back data for 20 seconds before being destroyed by a huge dust storm.

🪐 *Viking 1* **sent back the first colour pictures** from Mars in July 1976.

🪐 **The aim of the Viking missions** was to find signs of life, but there were none. Even so, the Viking landers sent back plenty of information about the geology and atmosphere of Mars.

▼ *The Viking landers took soil samples from Mars in 1976, but found no signs of life.*

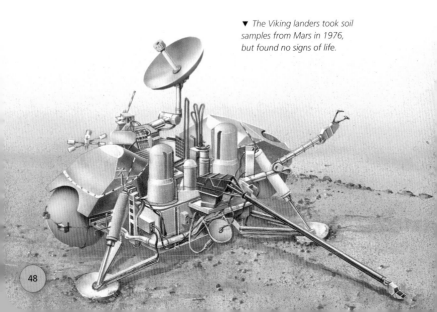

🪐 **On 4 July 1997,** the US *Mars Pathfinder* probe arrived on Mars and sent back 'live' pictures from the surface of the planet.

🪐 *Mars Pathfinder* **carried** the first robot vehicle to Mars. Called *Sojourner*, it inched slowly across the rocky surface taking measurements of the soil and rocks.

🪐 **Two robots called the Mars Exploration rovers,** *Spirit* and *Opportunity*, arrived on the red planet in January 2004.

🪐 **They travelled across the surface,** navigating their way around rocks and craters using onboard cameras.

▼ Mars Pathfinder *carried a small rover,* Sojourner, *to Mars in 1997. The rover collected samples for three months.*

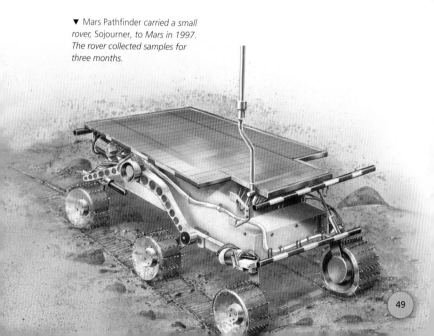

Mission to Mars

▼ An artist's impression of a future Mars landing. With their spacecraft in orbit, astronauts would descend to the planet's surface in an excursion vehicle. This would later carry them back into orbit to rendezvous with their spacecraft.

A manned mission to Mars is possible with existing technology, but it would be extremely expensive. Current estimates of the cost vary from $10 billion to $450 billion (£6.7 billion to £303 billion).

Astronauts who visit Mars would face many hazards. They would be exposed to high-energy cosmic rays during the 200-day journey and they would have to avoid the Martian dust-storm season, which lasts 14 Earth months.

Radio messages can take as long as 18 minutes to travel between Earth and Mars, so the Martian astronauts would experience considerable communications lag if they needed the assistance of Earth-based mission controllers during an emergency.

There is a difference of opinion about the best way to get a Mars mission off the ground. One suggestion is to use a single large launch vehicle, such as the proposed *Ares V*, to put a Mars spacecraft into orbit around the Earth.

An alternate suggestion is to load the components of the Mars spacecraft aboard a number of smaller and cheaper launch vehicles, and then assemble them in orbit.

A joint American-European mission has been proposed that would use two spacecraft – one to carry six astronauts and the other to carry their supplies and equipment. The mission would take about 450 days, with three astronauts spending 60 days on the surface of Mars.

The earliest date of a manned Mars mission is very unlikely to be before 2037, by which time robot spacecraft will likely already have brought samples of Martian soil and rocks back to Earth.

Astronomy

Astronomy

🪐 **The study of the night sky** is called astronomy – from the planets and moons to the stars and galaxies.

🪐 **Astronomy is the most ancient** of all the sciences, dating back at least 5000 years.

🪐 **The ancient Egyptians used their knowledge** of astronomy to work out their calendar and to align the pyramids.

🪐 **The word 'astronomy'** comes from the ancient Greek words *astro* meaning 'star', and *nomia* meaning 'law'.

🪐 **Astronomers use telescopes** to study objects that are too faint and small to be seen with the naked eye.

🪐 **Space objects give out** other kinds of radiation besides light. Astronomers have special equipment to detect this (see radio and space telescopes).

🪐 **Professional astronomers** usually study photographs and computer displays instead of staring through telescopes because many space objects only show up on long-exposure photographs.

🪐 **Astronomers can spot new objects** in the night sky by laying a current photograph over an old one and looking for differences.

🪐 **Professional astronomy involves** sophisticated equipment, but amateurs can occasionally make important discoveries.

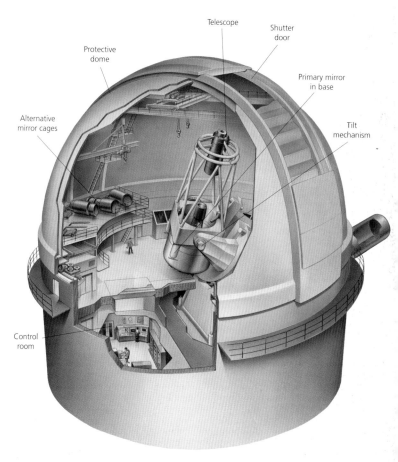

Telescope

Shutter door

Protective dome

Primary mirror in base

Tilt mechanism

Alternative mirror cages

Control room

▲ The telescope is protected by a large dome, which opens to let the telescope point at the sky.

The night sky

🪐 **The night sky is brightened** by the Moon and twinkling points of light.

🪐 **Most lights in the sky** are stars. Moving, flashing lights may be satellites.

🪐 **The brightest 'stars'** in the night sky are not actually stars at all, but the planets, Jupiter, Venus and Mars.

🪐 **About 2000 stars** can be seen with the naked eye.

🪐 **The pale band across** the middle of the sky is a side-on view of our galaxy, the Milky Way.

🪐 **The pattern of stars** in the sky is fixed, but seems to rotate (turn) through the night sky as the Earth spins.

🪐 **It takes 23 hours and 56 minutes** for the star pattern to return to the same place in the sky.

🪐 **As Earth orbits the Sun**, our view of the stars changes and the pattern starts in a different place each night.

🪐 **Different patterns of stars** are seen in the Northern Hemisphere and the Southern Hemisphere.

DID YOU KNOW?
The Andromeda Galaxy is over 2.2 million light years away, but can be seen clearly with the naked eye.

▲ *About 2000 stars can be seen twinkling in the sky. Stars twinkle because of the shimmering of heat in the Earth's atmosphere. Some of the stars are trillions of kilometres away and their light takes thousands of years to reach us.*

Star patterns

🪐 **Seeing patterns** in the arrangement of stars in the sky is undoubtedly very ancient and predates civilization, but the first evidence of named constellations comes from Mesopotamia (modern Iraq) in about 3000 BC.

🪐 **The Mesopotamians named** some of their constellations after animals, for example 'the lion', and others after occupations, such as 'the herdsman'.

🪐 **Ancient Egyptians interpreted** the constellations as representing their gods and goddesses. The modern constellation Draco was the hippopotamus-headed goddess Tawaret, while Ursa Major was seen as a jackal, symbolizing the god Set.

🪐 **Ancient Chinese astronomers arranged** the night sky in an entirely different manner. The stars were grouped into 28 lunar mansions that were divided into four groups – the Red Bird of the south, the Black Tortoise of the north, the Blue Dragon of the east and the White Tiger of the west.

🪐 **The individual mansions** had names that were mostly taken from everyday life, such as the Encampment, the Roof, the Room, and the Winnowing-basket – although the ancient Chinese knew the modern constellation of Cancer as the Ghost.

🪐 **In ancient India**, astronomers arranged the night sky into 27 divisions that were known as nakshratras. Each nakshratra was centred on a particular star or planet and was associated with a certain god or goddess.

🪐 **In Australia,** under clear desert skies, the Aborigines interpreted the night sky in an entirely different manner – they saw pictures and patterns in the areas of relative darkness between the stars.

🪐 **Easily identifiable patterns of stars** that do not form a whole constellation are called asterisms. The most famous asterism is the Big Dipper (which in Britain is known as the Plough) that forms part of Ursa Major.

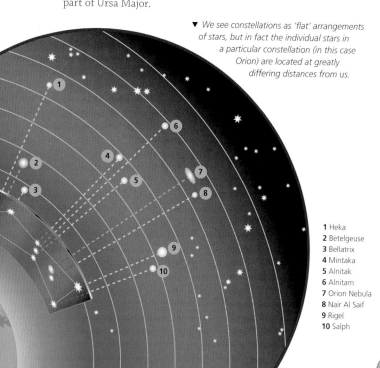

▼ *We see constellations as 'flat' arrangements of stars, but in fact the individual stars in a particular constellation (in this case Orion) are located at greatly differing distances from us.*

1 Heka
2 Betelgeuse
3 Bellatrix
4 Mintaka
5 Alnitak
6 Alnitam
7 Orion Nebula
8 Nair Al Saif
9 Rigel
10 Salph

Zodiac

- **The zodiac is the band of constellations** that the Sun appears to pass in front of during the year as the Earth orbits the Sun. It lies along the ecliptic.

- **The ecliptic is the plane** of the Earth's orbit around the Sun. The Moon and all the planets, except dwarf planet Pluto, lie in on this plane.

- **The ancient Greeks divided** the zodiac into 12 parts, named after the constellation they saw in each part. These are the signs of the zodiac.

- **The 12 constellations of the zodiac** are Capricorn, Aquarius, Pisces, Aries, Taurus, Gemini, Cancer, Leo, Virgo, Libra, Scorpio and Sagittarius.

- **Astrologers believe** that the movements of the planets and stars in the zodiac affect people's lives.

- **For astrologers**, all the constellations of the zodiac are equal in size.

- **The Earth has tilted** slightly since ancient times and the constellations no longer correspond to the zodiac.

- **The Moon and planets** stay within the band of the zodiac as they move across the sky.

- **The dates that the Sun** seems to pass in front of each constellation no longer match the dates astrologers use.

▼ *The zodiac signs are imaginary symbols that ancient astronomers linked to star patterns.*

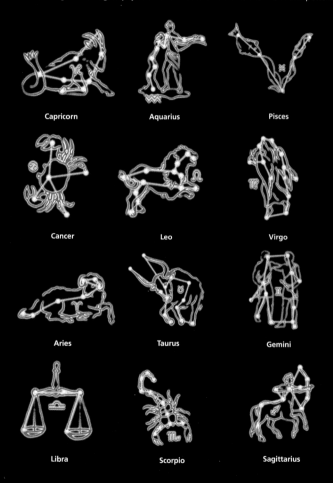

Capricorn

Aquarius

Pisces

Cancer

Leo

Virgo

Aries

Taurus

Gemini

Libra

Scorpio

Sagittarius

The Milky Way

- **On clear, dark nights**, the Milky Way can be seen as a pale glowing band that stretches right across the sky.

- **The Romans were the first** to use the phrase Milky Way (Via Lactea). The ancient Greek astronomers called it the Milky Circle (Kiklos Galaxias).

▼ *A small telescope will reveal some of the countless millions of stars that make up the Milky Way.*

- **According to Greek myth**, the goddess Hera produced the milk in the Milky Circle to feed the infant hero Hercules.

- **Some Native American peoples** regarded the Milky Way as the route taken by ghosts on their way to the land of the hereafter.

- **The Inuit peoples of Alaska** and northern Canada saw the Milky Way as a pathway of glowing ashes that led weary travellers home.

- **For Aborigines**, the patches of darkness in the Milky Way made a picture of a giant emu stretching across the heavens.

- **Seventh-century Korean astronomers** marked the position of stars with black dots on white paper and they showed the Milky Way as a thick black band.

- **Galileo was the first astronomer** to observe the Milky Way through a telescope and discover its true nature as 'congeries of innumerable stars'.

- **The German philosopher Emmanuel Kant** (1724–1804) was the first to speculate that if the Milky Way was a galaxy of stars, then there might be other, more distant, 'Milky Ways' visible in the night sky.

- **The astronomer William Herschel** was the first to draw a map of what the Milky Way might look like if viewed from the outside. His disc-shaped image became known as the 'grindstone' model.

- **By studying** the distribution of globular clusters in the Milky Way, the American astronomer Harlow Shapely (1885–1972) was able to deduce that the Sun was located near the edge of the Milky Way.

Space catalogues

- **Astronomers list the stars** in each constellation according to their brightness, using the Greek alphabet (see constellations).

- **The first catalogue of non-stellar objects** (things other than stars, such as nebulae) was made by astronomer Charles Messier (1730–1817). Objects were named 'M' (for Messier) plus a number.

- **Messier published a list** of 103 objects in 1781. The final catalogue lists 110 galaxies, nebulae and star clusters.

- **Many of the objects** originally listed by Messier as nebulae are now known to be galaxies.

- **Today the standard list** of non-stellar objects is the New General Catalogue of nebulae and star clusters (NGC). First published in 1888, this soon ran to over 13,000 entries.

- **Many objects** are in both the Messier and the NGC and therefore have two numbers. The Andromeda Galaxy is M31 and NGC 224.

- **Radio sources** are listed in similar catalogues, such as Cambridge University's 3C catalogue.

- **The first quasar** to be discovered was 3C 273.

- **Many pulsars** are now listed according to their position by right ascension and declination (see celestial sphere).

▶ *With such an infinite number of stars, galaxies and nebulae in the night sky, astronomers need very detailed catalogues to locate each object reliably and check whether it has already been investigated.*

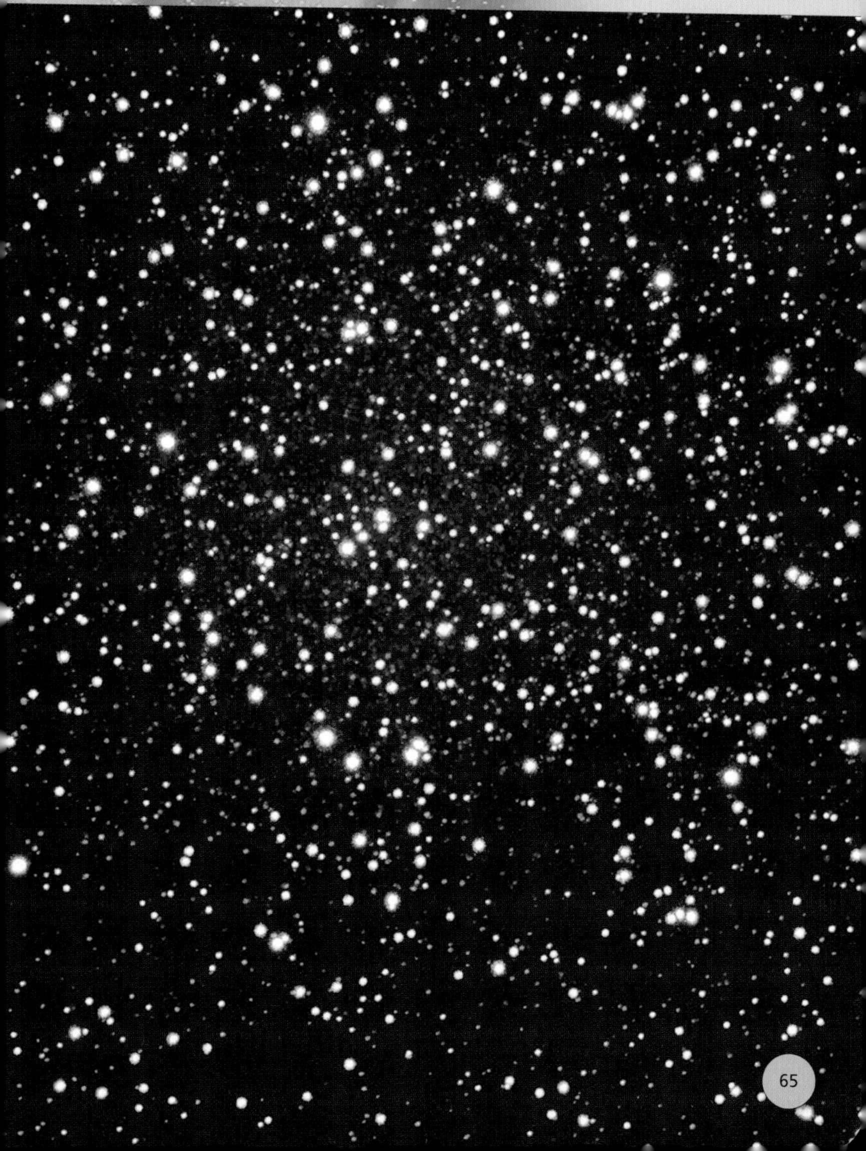

Telescopes

- **Optical telescopes magnify distant objects** using lenses or mirrors to focus light rays, which makes an enlarged image of the object.

- **Other telescopes detect** radio waves (see radio telescopes), X-rays (see X-rays) or other kinds of electromagnetic radiation (see radiation).

- **Refracting telescopes** are optical telescopes that use lenses to refract (bend) the light rays.

- **Reflecting telescopes** are optical telescopes that focus light rays by reflecting them off curved mirrors.

- **Reflecting telescopes bend the light rays** back on themselves so they are shorter than refracting rays.

- **Most professional astronomers** do not gaze at the stars directly, but pick up what the telescope shows with light sensors called Charge-Coupled Devices (CCDs).

- **Most early discoveries** in astronomy were made with refracting telescopes.

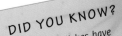

DID YOU KNOW?

Telescope dishes have to be made accurate to within about 10 billionths of a metre.

Platform for observation

🪐 **Modern observatories use** gigantic reflector dishes made up of hexagons of glass or coated metal.

🪐 **Large telescope dishes** are continually monitored and tweaked by computers to make sure that the reflector's mirrored surface stays completely smooth.

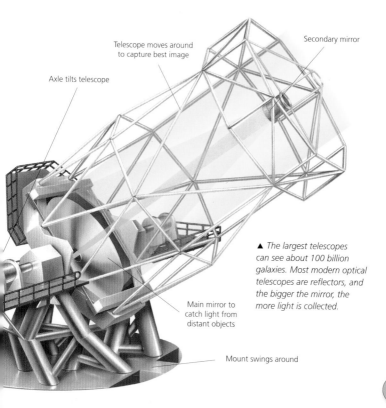

Telescope moves around to capture best image

Secondary mirror

Axle tilts telescope

Main mirror to catch light from distant objects

Mount swings around

▲ The largest telescopes can see about 100 billion galaxies. Most modern optical telescopes are reflectors, and the bigger the mirror, the more light is collected.

Observatories

🪐 **Astronomers study space in observatories**. To give the best view of the night sky, most are built on mountain tops far from city lights.

🪐 **One of the largest observatory complexes** is 4200 m above sea level, in the crater of the extinct Hawaiian volcano, Mauna Kea.

🪐 **In most observatories**, telescopes are housed in a domed building, which turns around so the telescopes can be aimed at the same stars while the Earth rotates.

🪐 **The oldest existing observatory** is thought to be a prehistoric circle built about 7000 years ago in Goseck, Germany.

🪐 **At the Beijing Ancient Observatory**, China, there are 500-year-old bronze astronomical instruments.

🪐 **The first British observatory** was the Royal Greenwich Observatory, London, founded in 1675.

🪐 **The highest observatory** on Earth is 4517 m above sea level, at Hanle, India, in the Himalayas.

🪐 **The lowest observatory** is 1.7 km below sea level, in Homestake Mine, South Dakota, USA. Its 'telescope' is actually tanks of heavy water that trap neutrinos from the Sun (see cosmic rays).

The first photographs of the stars were taken in 1840. Today, most observatories rely on photographs rather than on the eyes of astronomers.

Observatory photographs are made using CCDs, which give off an electrical signal when struck by light.

◀ *The Kitt Peak National Observatory in Arizona, USA.*

Spectra and emission lines

🪐 **Light from the Sun**, stars and other sources can be studied using an instrument called a spectrograph, attached to the viewing end of a telescope.

🪐 **The spectrograph has** a very small, slit-like aperture at the telescope's point of focus so that only the light from a particular source enters the instrument.

🪐 **Inside the spectrograph**, a device called a collimator turns the cone of light into parallel rays and these are then split into a spectrum by a glass prism.

🪐 **A spectrum with more blue than red** indicates a very hot star, such as a white dwarf, while a spectrum with more red than blue indicates a large, fairly cool star such as a red giant.

🪐 **Each of the chemical elements** absorbs and emits light at very precise wavelengths and these produce spectral lines that can be used to identify the different elements present in a star.

🪐 **The presence of dark absorption lines** superimposed on a continuous spectrum shows that some of the light has been absorbed on its way to Earth. For example, carbon absorption lines may indicate that the light has passed through a cloud of interstellar dust.

DID YOU KNOW?

A continuous spectrum of colours is produced by the hot, dense surface of a star such as the Sun.

▲ *The solar observatory at Kitt Peak, Arizona, USA, is equipped with a rotating mirror that reflects sunlight down a 152-m-sloping tunnel to an underground spectrograph.*

🪐 **Clouds of high-temperature**, low-pressure gas, such as nebulae, produce a spectrum that consists only of a series of bright emission lines.

🪐 **Wide emission lines indicate** a rapidly rotating or expanding gas that may have been produced by a supernova.

🪐 **Astronomers also study spectra** at wavelengths other than that of visible light. In radio astronomy, the 21-cm-long hydrogen line is particularly important because hydrogen is by far the most abundant element in the Universe.

Radio telescopes

- **Radio telescopes are used** to pick up radio waves instead of light waves.

- **Radio telescopes**, like reflecting telescopes (see telescopes), have a big dish to collect and focus data.

- **At the centre of its dish**, a radio telescope has an antenna to pick up radio signals.

- **Radio waves are much longer** than light waves, so radio telescope dishes are very big, up to 100 m across.

- **Instead of one big dish**, some radio telescopes use a collection of small, linked dishes. The further apart the dishes are, the sharper the image.

- **The Very Long Baseline Array** (VLBA) is made of ten dishes scattered across the USA.

- **Radio astronomy** led to the discovery of pulsars and background radiation from the Big Bang.

- **Radio galaxies are very distant** and only faintly visible (if at all), but they can be detected because they give out radio waves.

- **Radio astronomy proved** that the Milky Way is a disc-shaped galaxy with spiralling arms.

DID YOU KNOW?

At 305 m across, the Arecibo radio telescope in Puerto Rico is the largest dish telescope in the world.

◀ *Many radio telescopes use an array of dishes linked by a process called interferometry.*

Space telescopes

🪐 **In order to study the Universe** without interference from the Earth's atmosphere, space telescopes are launched as satellites.

🪐 **The first space telescope** was Uhuru, sent up in 1970.

🪐 **The most famous space telescope** is the Hubble, launched from the space shuttle in 1990.

🪐 **Different space telescopes** study all the different forms of radiation that make up the electromagnetic spectrum (see light).

🪐 **The COBE and WMAP satellites** picked up microwave radiation that was left over from the Big Bang.

🪐 **The ISO and Spitzer observatories** studied infrared radiation from objects as small as space dust.

🪐 **Space telescopes that have studied** ultraviolet rays from the stars include the International Ultraviolet Explorer (IUE) and the Extreme Ultraviolet Explorer (EUVE).

🪐 **The Solar and Heliospheric Observatory** (SOHO) was one of many space telescopes studying the Sun.

🪐 **X-rays can only be picked up** by certain space telescopes such as Chandra and XMM.

🪐 **Gamma rays can only be detected** by particular space telescopes such as the Compton Gamma Ray Observatory.

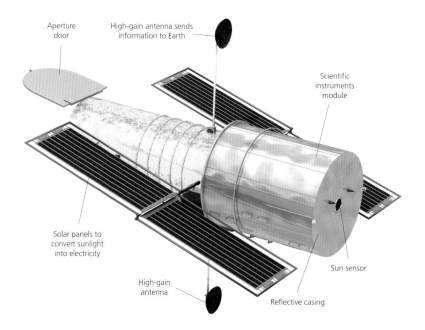

Aperture door

High-gain antenna sends information to Earth

Scientific instruments module

Solar panels to convert sunlight into electricity

Sun sensor

High-gain antenna

Reflective casing

▲ The Hubble space telescope can detect clear images of faint objects in space because it is above the Earth's atmosphere.

Hipparchus

- **Hipparchus of Nicaea** was a Greek astronomer who lived in the 2nd century BC, and died in 127 BC.

- **The framework for astronomy** was created by Hipparchus.

- **Hipparchus' ideas** were almost lost until they were rescued by Greek astronomer, Ptolemy. They were developed into a system that lasted 1500 years until they were overthrown by the ideas of Copernicus.

- **Ancient Babylonian records** brought back by Alexander the Great from his conquests helped Hipparchus to make his observations of the stars.

◄ Hipparchus carried out his observations at Rhodes. He was the first to pinpoint the geographical position of places by latitude and longitude.

▲ *Some of Hipparchus' knowledge of stars came from the Sumerians, who wrote on clay tablets.*

🪐 **Hipparchus was the first astronomer** to measure Earth's distance to the Sun.

🪐 **The first star catalogue**, listing 850 stars, was put together by Hipparchus.

🪐 **Hipparchus was also the first to identify** the constellations systematically and to assess stars in terms of magnitude (see star brightness).

🪐 **Hipparchus discovered** that the positions of the stars on the equinoxes (21 March and 23 September) slowly shift around, taking 26,000 years to return to their original place. This is the 'precession of the equinoxes'.

DID YOU KNOW?
The mathematics of trigonometry is thought to have been invented by Hipparchus.

Ptolemy

🪐 **The most famous of the ancient astronomers** was Ptolemy. He revived, extended, and publicized the work of earlier Greek astronomers, especially Hipparchus.

🪐 **Ptolemy lived and worked** in the city of Alexandria during the first half of the 2nd century AD. According to tradition he died there in AD 151 at the age of 78.

🪐 **Ptolemy's astronomical work** was published in a book entitled *The Mathematical Collection*, but which became known in Greek as *The Great Astronomer*.

🪐 **Islamic scholars of the Middle Ages** referred to his book as the *Megiste* (*Masterwork*), and it is now generally known as the *Almagest*.

🪐 **The *Almagest* is divided into 13 chapters**. The first six chapters are concerned with the motion of the Sun and Moon. Chapters seven and eight deal with the stars and the constellations and the final five chapters are about the planets.

🪐 **Ptolemy followed Hipparchus in believing** that the Earth was at the centre of the Universe, and this Ptolemaic viewpoint lasted until the Copernican Revolution overthrew it.

🪐 **Ptolemy also believed** that the Sun, stars and planets were embedded in series of concentric transparent crystal spheres that surrounded the Earth.

🪐 **According to Ptolemy**, the sequence of heavenly bodies from the Earth outwards was: the Moon, Mercury, Venus, the Sun, Mars, Jupiter, Saturn and the stars.

▲ *Ptolemy's conception of the Universe, with the Earth at the centre, was accepted for more than 1000 years until overturned by the Copernican Revolution.*

🪐 **Ptolemy extended Hipparchus' star catalogue** to include a total of 1022 stars and defined 48 of the constellations that are now internationally recognized.

🪐 **In a separate book he prepared** a calendar showing the times of rising and setting of certain prominent stars during morning and evening twilight.

Islamic astronomers

🪐 **During the so-called 'Dark Ages'** that followed the collapse of the Roman empire in Europe, the learning of the ancient Greek astronomers was kept alive by Islamic scholars in the Arab empire.

🪐 **The oldest surviving hemispheric star map**, which shows about 400 stars, decorates the domed roof of a palace that was constructed in Jordan towards the end of the 7th century AD.

🪐 **Having defeated the Byzantine empire** in battle, the 9th-century Islamic ruler Al- Ma'mun demanded a copy of Ptolemy's *Almagest* as one of his conditions for making peace.

🪐 **Al-Ma'mun arranged for the *Almagest*** to be translated into Arabic and had copies placed in the library of the House of Wisdom that he established in Baghdad.

🪐 **The most famous of the Islamic astronomers** was Abd al-Rahman Ibn Umar al-Sufi (903–986), who produced a *Book of Fixed Stars* that combined Ptolemy's work with traditional Arab star lore.

🪐 **Many of the stars had traditional Arabic names**, such as bright red Algol (the demon) and Aldebaran (the follower), which appears to follow the Pleiades across the sky.

🪐 **Although Al-Sufi accepted** Ptolemy's positions for the stars, he revised the table of magnitudes (brightness) according to his own observations.

🪐 **Islamic astronomers** in the Middle East and Spain produced the first portable celestial globes (made from brass and silver) during the 11th century.

🪐 **Ulugh Beg**, who was the grandson of the great conqueror Timor (Tamerlane), was the first Islamic astronomer to systematically re-observe all the stars listed by Ptolemy.

🪐 **In order to get accurate observations** Ulugh Beg built a huge observatory at Samarkand, Uzbekistan, which was equipped with a stone sextant that measured about 50 m in length.

▼ *In the Middle Ages, astronomers and explorers used small metal astrolabes to measure the angles between stars.*

Copernicus

◄ *'The Earth,'* wrote Copernicus, *'carrying the Moon's path, passes in a great orbit among the other planets in an annual revolution around the Sun.'*

🐚 **Until the 16th century** most people thought the Earth was the centre of the Universe and that everything – the Moon, Sun, planets and stars – revolved around it.

🐚 **Nicolaus Copernicus** (1473–1543) was the astronomer who first suggested that the Sun was the centre, and that the Earth went around the Sun. This is called the heliocentric view.

🐚 **Copernicus had an extensive education** at the best universities in Poland and Italy. He studied astronomy, astrology, medicine and law.

🐚 **In his book**, *De revolutionibus orbium coelestium* (On the Revolutions of the Heavenly Spheres), Copernicus described his ideas.

🐚 **The Roman Catholic Church** banned Copernicus' book for about 140 years.

- **Copernicus' ideas** didn't come from looking at the night sky, but from studying ancient astronomy.

- **Copernicus' main clue** came from the way the planets seem to perform a backward loop through the sky every now and then.

- **The first proof of Copernicus' theory** came in 1610, when Galileo saw, through a telescope, moons revolving around Jupiter.

- **The change in ideas** that was brought about by Copernicus is known as the Copernican Revolution.

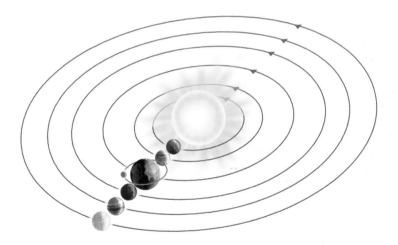

▲ *Copernicus was the first to realize that the Sun is at the centre of the Solar System, and the planets orbit around it.*

Galileo

🪐 **Galileo Galilei** (1564–1642)
was a great Italian mathematician and
astronomer.

🪐 **The pendulum clock** was invented by Galileo after he saw
a swinging lamp in Pisa Cathedral in 1583.

🪐 **Galileo's experiments with balls** rolling down slopes laid the
basis for our understanding of how gravity makes things accelerate
(speed up).

🪐 **When the telescope was invented**, Galileo made his own
telescope to look at the Moon, Venus and Jupiter.

🪐 **Galileo described his observations** of space in a book called
The Starry Messenger, published in 1610.

🪐 **Through his telescope**, Galileo saw that Jupiter has four moons
(see Jupiter's Galilean moons). He also saw that Venus has phases
(as the Earth's Moon does).

🪐 **Jupiter's moons and Venus' phases** were the first visible
evidence of Copernicus' theory that the Earth moves around the
Sun. Galileo also believed this.

🪐 **Galileo supported the Copernican theory**, which was declared
a heresy by the Catholic Church in 1616. Later, threatened with
torture, Galileo was forced to deny that the Earth orbits the Sun.
Legend has it he muttered *'eppur si muove'* (yet it does move)
afterwards.

▲ The Galileo probe was sent to Jupiter in 1995 and
sent back images of the planet and its moons.

Kepler

🪐 **German astronomer, Johannes Kepler** (1571–1630), discovered the basic rules about the way in which the planets move.

🪐 **Kepler got his ideas** from studying the movement of Mars.

🪐 **Before Kepler's discoveries**, it was thought that the planets moved in circles.

🪐 **Kepler discovered** that the true shape of the planets' orbits is elliptical (oval). This is Kepler's first law.

🪐 **Kepler's second law** is that the speed of a planet through space varies according to its distance from the Sun.

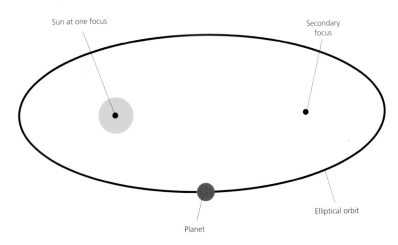

Sun at one focus

Secondary focus

Elliptical orbit

Planet

▲ Kepler discovered that planets have an elliptical orbit around the Sun. The Sun is not at the centre, but at one of the focuses.

► Despite almost losing his eyesight and the use of his hands through smallpox at the age of three, Johannes Kepler became an assistant to the great Danish atronomer Tycho Brahe, and took over his work when Brahe died.

DID YOU KNOW?

Kepler also wrote a book on how to measure the amount of wine in wine casks. This proved to be important for the mathematics of calculus.

🪐 **A planet moves fastest** when its orbit brings it nearest to the Sun (its perihelion). It moves slowest when it is furthest from the Sun (its aphelion).

🪐 **The third law** is that a planet's period (the time it takes to complete its yearly orbit of the Sun) depends on its distance from the Sun.

🪐 **Kepler's third law states** that the square of a planet's period is proportional to the cube of its average distance from the Sun.

🪐 **He also believed** that the planets made music as they moved called 'the music of the spheres'.

Newton

🪐 **Isaac Newton** (1642–1727) discovered the force of gravity and the three basic laws of motion.

🪐 **Newton's discovery of gravity** showed why planets orbit the Sun.

🪐 **He realized** that a planet's orbit depends on its mass and its distance from the Sun.

🪐 **The further apart** and the lighter two objects are, the weaker the pull of gravity is between them.

DID YOU KNOW?

Newton's ideas were inspired by seeing an apple fall from a tree in the garden of his home.

White light

Spectrum of colours

Prism

▲ Newton also discovered that sunlight can be split into a spectrum made of all the colours of the rainbow.

◀ *Newton was made Lucasian professor of mathematics at Cambridge University in 1669, where he studied how and why things in our Universe move.*

● **To calculate the pull of gravity** between two objects, multiply their masses together, then divide the total by the square of the distance between them.

● **This calculation allows astronomers** to predict precisely the movement of every planet, star and galaxy in the Universe.

● **Using Newton's formula for gravity**, astronomers have detected unknown stars and planets, including Neptune, from the effect of their gravity on other space objects.

● **Newton's three laws of motion** showed that every movement in the Universe can be calculated mechanically.

89

Herschel

🪐 **William Herschel** (1739–1822) was a German musician who became the King's astronomer in England and built his own powerful telescopes.

🪐 **Until Herschel's time**, astronomers thought that there were only five planets, in addition to Earth, orbiting the Sun.

🪐 **The five known planets** at that time were Mercury, Venus, Mars, Jupiter and Saturn.

🪐 **Uranus, the sixth planet**, was discovered by William Herschel in 1781.

🪐 **At first Herschel thought** that the dot of light he could see through his telescope was a nebula or comet. When he looked again four days later, it had moved against the background of stars, so it must be in the Solar System. He realized that it was a new planet.

🪐 **He wanted to name** the planet George, after King George III, but Uranus was eventually chosen, after the ancient Greek god of the sky.

▶ William Herschel was one of the greatest astronomers. With the help of his sister, Caroline, he discovered Uranus in 1781. He later identified two of the moons of Uranus and two of Saturn.

▶ The huge, extremely powerful telescope that Herschel built at his own home, in Bath, England.

🪐 **His sister, Caroline** (1750–1848), was his partner in his discoveries. She was a great astronomer who discovered eight comets and produced catalogues of stars and nebulae.

🪐 **John, Herschel's son**, catalogued the stars of the Southern Hemisphere.

🪐 **Herschel himself added** to the catalogue of nebulae.

91

Einstein

 The great scientist, Albert Einstein (1879–1955), is known for uncovering the two theories of relativity.

 Special relativity shows that all measurements are relative, including time and speed. In other words, time and speed depend on where they are measured.

 The fastest thing in the Universe, light, always travels at the same speed, no matter where you are or how fast you are going. Nothing can travel faster than light.

 Special relativity shows that as things travel faster, they seem to become shorter and heavier.

 The theory of general relativity includes the idea of special relativity, but also describes how gravity works.

 General relativity predicts that light rays from stars will be bent by the gravitational pull of the stars they pass.

 Gravity bends light rays simply by stretching space (and time).

 Einstein overturned the idea that time is the same everywhere. He was the first to show that time is relative.

 Time is not fixed but depends entirely on how you measure it – and you can only measure it relative to something else.

▶ *Einstein's theory of general relativity was proved right in 1919, when light rays from a distant star just grazing the Sun were measured during an eclipse and shown to be bent.*

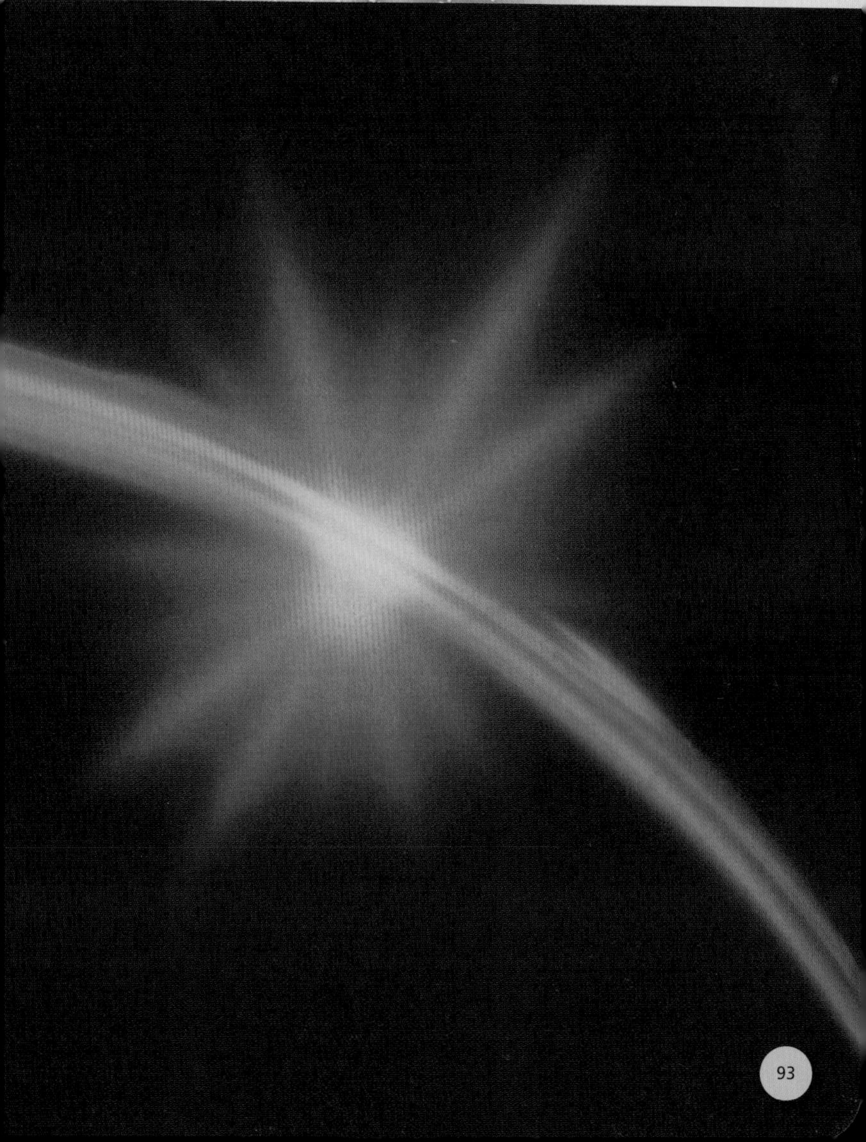

Hubble

- **Edwin Hubble** (1889–1953) was an American who trained in law at the Universities of Chicago and Oxford, and was also a great boxer before he turned to astronomy.

- **Until the early 20th century**, astronomers thought that the Milky Way galaxy was all there was in the Universe.

- **In the 1920s**, Hubble showed that the fuzzy patches of light once thought to be nebulae were in fact other galaxies far beyond the Milky Way.

- **In 1929, Hubble measured** the distances of 20 galaxies and showed that they were all moving away from the Earth.

- **Red shift showed Hubble** that the further away a galaxy is, the faster it is moving.

- **The ratio of a galaxy's distance** to the speed it is moving away from Earth is now known as Hubble's Law.

- **Hubble's Law** showed that the Universe is getting bigger and so must have started very small. This led to the idea of the Big Bang.

- **Hubble's constant is a measurement** of the rate at which the Universe is expanding.

- **In the 1930s, Hubble showed** that the Universe is isotropic (the same in all directions).

- **Hubble space telescope** is named after Edwin Hubble.

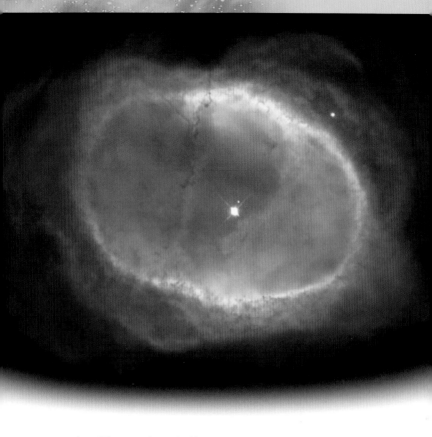

▲ *The Hubble space telescope is able to see space objects, such as planetary nebulae, in great detail.*

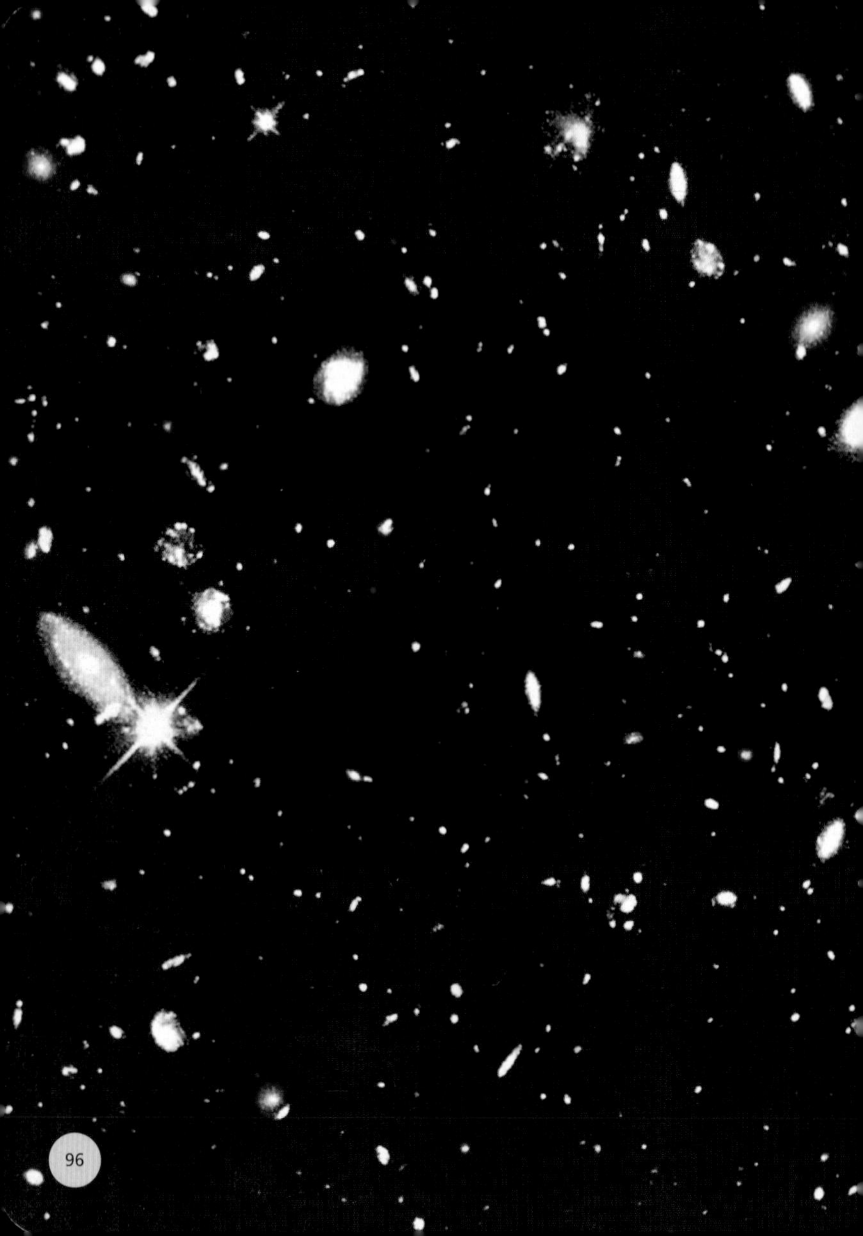

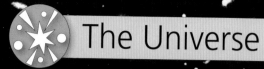

The Universe

The Universe

🌀 **The Universe** is everything that we can ever know – all of space and all of time. Before the Universe came into existence there was nothingness, no space, no time, no energy and no matter.

🌀 **The study** of the Universe, its history, future, and large-scale features is known as cosmology.

🌀 **Scientists believe** that the Universe started with an explosion known as the Big Bang. According to the latest estimates, the Universe is now about 14 billion years old.

🌀 **Since the Big Bang** the Universe has been expanding and continues to do so. The most distant galaxies are moving away from us at about 90 percent of the speed of light.

🌀 **The Universe** was once thought to be everything that could ever exist, but recent theories suggest that our Universe may just be one of countless bubbles of space-time.

🌀 **Although there is no maximum** possible temperature in the Universe, there is a very precise minimum possible temperature. The third law of thermodynamics states that it is impossible for anything to be cooled to absolute zero (–273°C).

🌀 **Working in specialized laboratories**, scientists have cooled substances to within a billionth of a degree of absolute zero, but they cannot achieve this ultimate low temperature.

🪐 **Matter is not distributed** evenly throughout the Universe. On the largest scale, the Universe consists of thin filaments, each one made up of millions of galaxies, which surround vast voids that contain nothing but clouds of intergalactic hydrogen.

🪐 **The largest structure** yet identified is an extended line of galaxies known as the Great Wall that is located about 500 million light years from our galaxy.

▼ *The Universe is getting bigger all the time as galaxies rush outwards in all directions.*

The Big Bang

🪐 **Events happened very quickly** at the beginning of the Universe. In order to explain what happened scientists use measurements of time that are as small as one ten million trillion trillion trillionth of a second.

🪐 **At first the Universe** was indescribably small and hot. It has been getting larger and cooler ever since.

🪐 **In its initial state**, the four fundamental forces (strong and weak nuclear forces, electromagnetism and gravity) were unified into a single force.

🪐 **Gravity was the first force** to separate, followed by the strong nuclear force. This triggered an event known as inflation and the Universe suddenly became billions of billions times bigger.

🪐 **About one-billionth of a second** after the Big Bang, the Universe consisted of a dense sea of quarks and other particles.

🪐 **About three minutes** after the Big Bang there was a brief period of nucleosynthesis when quarks joined together to form neutrons and protons.

🪐 **For the first 300,000 years** the Universe remained completely opaque. Then it became cool enough for protons and neutrons to capture electrons and form atoms.

🪐 **The Universe was now transparent** to light and other electromagnetic energy.

🪐 **About 100 million years** after the Big Bang, the first stars began to shine.

🪐 **There is still** much to be discovered about the Universe and the Big Bang.

🪐 **Scientists** have recently proposed that there must be a fifth fundamental force (known as dark energy or quintessence) that prevents the Universe from collapsing inwards under the force of its own gravity.

◄ The Big Bang fireball blasted out unimaginable amounts of energy, some of which eventually 'cooled' to produce the matter that formed the first galaxies.

Microwave background

- **The faint 'echoes' of the Big Bang** have been detected in the form of a cosmic microwave background radiation that pervades the whole Universe.

- **Background radiation** shows that the temperature of the Big Bang has now cooled to about 2.7°C above absolute zero.

- **American radio engineers** Arno Penzias and Robert Wilson discovered the microwave background in 1965, while trying to find the source of radio 'noise' that was interfering with communications.

- **At one time** they thought that pigeon droppings on their antennae might be causing the interference, but after a thorough cleaning the noise remained.

- **Eventually, they determined that the source** of the noise was located beyond the Milky Way galaxy, and that the signal appeared to be coming from all directions.

- **US physicist George Gamow predicted** the existence of microwave background radiation in 1947, although he believed it would be slightly warmer at around 10 degrees above absolute zero.

- **In 1993, the first images** of this radiation were produced by the Cosmic Background Explorer (COBE) spacecraft.

- **The COBE images** showed that the radiation was uniform to within one part in a thousand throughout the Universe, with minute ripples showing areas that were fractionally warmer or cooler.

🪐 **A subsequent survey** by instruments aboard the WMAP satellite has provided a more accurate picture that shows how the distribution of temperature fluctuations in the background radiation exactly mirrors the large-scale structure of the Universe.

🪐 **Slightly cooler regions were denser** and contained the matter that eventually condensed into the filaments of galaxies, while the slightly warmer regions became empty voids.

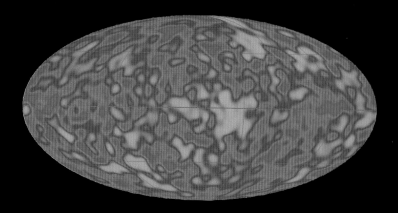

▲ *This image of the microwave background was obtained by the COBE spacecraft. It shows the minute variations in temperature (pink = warmer; blue = cooler) that were predicted by the Big Bang theorists.*

Objects

 The Universe consists of energy and matter irregularly distributed throughout the continuum of curving space-time, but most of the matter and energy is invisible to humans.

 Scientists now believe that the Universe is made up of 70 percent dark energy (see Big Bang), 27 percent dark matter, and about 3 percent ordinary 'luminous' matter in the form of stars and galaxies.

▼ *This bright galaxy is a single astronomical object, even though it contains billions of individual stars and is constantly forming new clusters of stars.*

- **The ordinary 'luminous' matter** is clumped together in objects of varying sizes and densities. The term 'object' refers to individual items that astronomers can examine through telescopes.

- **On Earth matter exists in three forms**, as gas, liquid and solid. There is a fourth form of matter – a completely ionized gas known as plasma – that can only be made in the laboratory.

- **Beyond Earth's atmosphere**, however, plasma is extremely common and is the main component of the 'wind' produced by stars and the intergalactic medium.

- **The largest astronomical objects** are galaxies, followed in terms of diminishing size by nebulas, stars, planets, moons, asteroids, comets and meteorites.

- **Although galaxies are made up of many billions of stars**, they are considered to be single objects. This is because their stars orbit around a common centre of gravity and have the same relative motion with respect to the rest of the Universe.

- **Astronomical objects** tend towards a spherical shape because the gravitational forces across the surface of a sphere are in equilibrium.

- **Rotation tends to distort spherical objects** into a discus-shape – the Earth, for example, bulges slightly around the Equator.

- **Objects of less than about 80 km** in diameter have insufficient mass to achieve a spherical shape, which is why the smaller asteroids all have irregular shapes.

Laws of nature

🌠 **Scientists can learn more about the Universe** by discovering the natural laws that govern the behaviour of matter and energy and the relationships between them.

🌠 **William of Occam**, an English philosopher, established the guiding principle behind natural laws. Known as 'Occam's Razor', this principle states that 'hypotheses should not be multiplied without reason', meaning that the simplest explanation is likely to be correct.

🌠 **In addition to his law of universal gravitation**, Isaac Newton also established three laws of motion that govern the movement of all objects larger than an atom, unless they are moving at close to the speed of light.

🌠 **Albert Einstein's theory of relativity** extended Newton's laws to include objects that are moving at near-light speed.

🌠 **Einstein's theory of relativity** led to his discovery that matter can be transformed into energy according to the famous equation $e=mc^2$, where 'e' is energy, 'm' is mass and 'c' is the speed of light.

🌠 **Four mathematical equations** devised by the Scottish physicist James Clerk Maxwell (1831–1879) describe phenomena associated with electricity and magnetism, and were used to predict the existence of the electromagnetic spectrum.

🌠 **In 1931**, the Indian astronomer Subramanyan Chandrasekhar proved that no white dwarf star could have a mass of more than 1.4 times the mass of the Sun. Any stars that exceed this mass will explode as supernovae rather than shrink to become white dwarfs.

According to Hubble's law, first stated by Edwin Hubble in 1929, the speed at which a galaxy appears to be moving away from us is proportional to its distance. The most distant galaxies are moving the fastest.

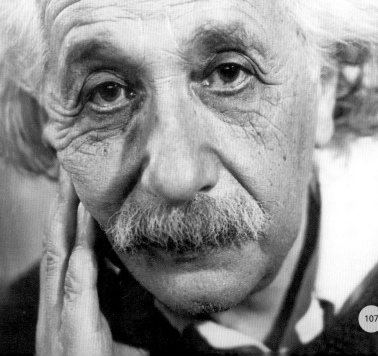

▼ *Albert Einstein revolutionized the way scientists view the Universe when he discovered some of the mathematical laws that govern the relationship between time and space, and energy and matter.*

Distances

- **The distance to the planets** is measured by bouncing radar signals off them and timing how long the signals take to get there and back.

- **Nearby stars'** distance is calculated by measuring the slight shift in the angle of each star in comparison to stars far away, as the Earth orbits the Sun. This is called parallax shift.

- **Parallax shift can only be used** to measure nearby stars, so astronomers work out the distance to faraway stars and galaxies by comparing how bright they look with how bright they actually are.

- **For middle distance stars**, astronomers compare colour with brightness using the Hertzsprung-Russell (H-R) diagram. This is called main sequence fitting.

- **Beyond 30,000 light years**, stars are too faint for main sequence fitting to work.

- **Distances to nearby galaxies** can be estimated using 'standard candles' – stars that astronomers know the brightness of, such as supergiants and supernovae.

- **The expected brightness** of a galaxy that is too far away to pick out its stars may be measured using the Tully-Fisher technique, based on how fast galaxies spin.

DID YOU KNOW?

A laser beam is used to measure the distance to the Moon.

🪐 **Counting planetary nebulae** (the rings of gas left behind by supernovae explosions) is another way of measuring how bright a distant galaxy should be.

🪐 **A third method** of calculating the brightness of a distant galaxy is to gauge how mottled it looks.

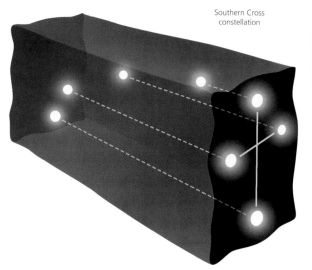

Southern Cross constellation

Side view of star pattern

▲ *From Earth, the stars in a constellation appear to be the same distance away. However, the relative distances between stars can be quite large.*

Light years

Distances in space are so vast that the fastest thing in the Universe, light, is used to measure them. The speed of light is about 300,000 km/sec.

▼ *Distances in space are so huge they are measured in light years – the distance light travels in a year.*

- **A light second is the distance** that light travels in one second – 300 million metres.

- **A light year is the distance** that light travels in one year – 9.46 trillion km.

- **Light years** are one of the standard distance measurements in astronomy.

- **It takes about eight minutes** for light from the Sun to reach Earth.

- **Light takes 4.22 years** to reach Earth from the Sun's nearest star, Proxima Centauri. This means the star is 4.22 light years away – more than 40 trillion km.

- **Viewed from Earth**, Proxima Centauri looks like it was 4.22 years ago because its light takes 4.22 years to reach Earth.

- **The star Deneb** is 1800 light years away, which means it looks like it was when Emperor Septimus Severius ruled Rome (AD 200).

- **Astronomers use parsecs** to measure distances. They originally came from parallax shift measurements (see distances). A light year is 0.3066 parsecs.

DID YOU KNOW?

With powerful telescopes, astronomers can see galaxies two billion light years away.

Light

⭐ **The fastest thing** in the Universe is light, which travels at 299,792,458 m/sec.

⭐ **Light rays always travel** in straight lines.

⭐ **As they pass from one material** to another, light rays change direction. This is called refraction.

⭐ **Colours are different wavelengths** of light.

⭐ **The longest light waves** that can be seen are red, and the shortest are violet.

DID YOU KNOW?

Photons of light travel in waves just 380–750 nanometres (millionths of a millimetre) in length.

▼ Light can be viewed as small packets of energy called photons. When a photon hits an atom, energy is produced as light, X-rays or radio waves.

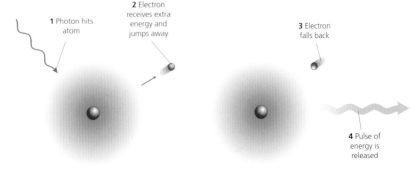

1 Photon hits atom

2 Electron receives extra energy and jumps away

3 Electron falls back

4 Pulse of energy is released

Atom

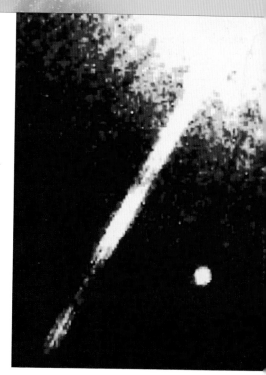

- **Light is a form** of electromagnetic radiation (see radiation). A light ray is a stream of tiny energy particles called photons.

- **Faint light from very distant stars** is often recorded by sensors called CCDs (see observatories). These count photons from the star as they arrive and build up a picture of the star over a long period.

- **The electromagnetic spectrum** includes radio waves, ultraviolet light and

▲ *Big nuclear reactions within stars cause them to emit vast amounts of light and other radiation.*

X-rays. Visible light is the only part of the spectrum that can be seen by the human eye.

- **All light is given out by atoms,** and atoms give out light when 'excited', perhaps by radiation.

Red shift

🪐 **When distant galaxies** are moving away from the Earth, the light waves they give off are stretched out behind them. This is because each bit of the light wave is being sent from a little further away.

🪐 **When the light waves** from distant galaxies are stretched out in this way, they look redder. This is called red shift.

🪐 **Red shift was first described** by Austrian mathematician Christian Doppler in 1842.

🪐 **Edwin Hubble showed** that a galaxy's red shift is proportional to its distance. The further away a galaxy is, the greater its red shift and the faster it must be zooming away from the Earth. This is known as Hubble's Law.

🪐 **The increase of red shift** with distance proved that the Universe is growing bigger.

🪐 **Only nearby galaxies** show no red shift at all.

🪐 **The most distant galaxies** have red shifts of up to seven.

🪐 **Red shift can be caused** by the expansion of the Universe, gravity or the effect of relativity (see Einstein).

🪐 **Black holes may create** large red shifts.

▶ *Massive red shifts reveal that the most distant objects in the Universe are flying away from the Earth at astonishing speeds – often approaching the speed of light.*

Radiation

- **The energy that is given out** by atoms at high speed is called radiation. There are two main forms – atomic particles and electromagnetic radiation.

- **Electromagnetic radiation either travels** as waves or as tiny particles called photons (see light).

- **Radioactivity is where an atom decays** (breaks down) and sends out gamma rays and particles.

- **Nuclear radiation is generated** by atomic bombs and nuclear power stations.

- **Electromagnetic radiation** is electric and magnetic fields that move in tiny bursts of waves, or photons.

- **There are different kinds** of electromagnetic radiation, each with different wavelengths.

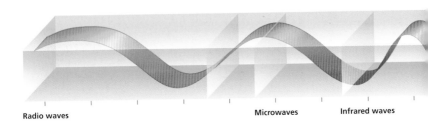

Radio waves   Microwaves   Infrared waves

- **Gamma rays are a very short-wave**, energetic and dangerous form of electromagnetic radiation.

- **Radio waves are a long-wave**, low-energy radiation.

- **In between gamma rays and radio waves** are X-rays, ultraviolet rays, visible light, infrared rays and microwaves.

- **Together, these forms of electromagnetic radiation** are called the electromagnetic spectrum.

- **All electromagnetic rays** move at the speed of light – 299,792,458 m/sec.

- **Everything that can be detected in space** is picked up by the radiation that it gives out.

▼ *Visible light is the only part of the electromagnetic spectrum that can be seen with the human eye.*

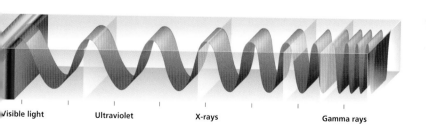

Visible light   Ultraviolet   X-rays   Gamma rays

Nuclear energy

- **The energy that holds** the nucleus of every atom together is called nuclear energy.

- **Nuclear energy fuels** nuclear power stations, and every star in the Universe. It can be released either by fission or fusion.

▼ The extraordinary power locked in the nucleus of atoms is shown when the explosion of a nuclear bomb releases some of the energy.

- **Nuclear fusion occurs when nuclear energy** is released as nuclei join together. This occurs inside stars when they are squeezed together by gravity.

- **Usually only tiny nuclei**, such as those of hydrogen and helium, fuse (join). Only under extreme pressure in huge, exploding stars do big nuclei, such as those of iron, fuse.

DID YOU KNOW?

The Hiroshima bomb released 84 trillion joules of energy. A supernova releases 125,000 trillion trillion times as much.

- **Nuclear fission occurs when nuclear energy** is released by the splitting of nuclei. This is the method used in most power stations and in atomic bombs.

- **Nuclear fission involves** splitting big nuclei, such as Uranium-235 and plutonium.

- **When a nucleus splits**, it gives out gamma rays, neutrons (see atoms) and intense heat.

- **In an atomic bomb**, the energy is released in one second.

- **In a power station**, control rods ensure that nuclear reactions are slowed down to release energy gradually.

X-rays

- **X-rays are electromagnetic rays** with waves shorter than ultraviolet rays and longer than gamma rays.

- **In space, X-rays may be produced** by very hot gases more than one million°C.

- **X-rays are also made** when electrons interact with a magnetic field in synchrotron radiation (see cosmic rays).

- **As X-rays cannot get through** the Earth's atmosphere, astronomers can only detect the rays using space telescopes, such as ROSAT, Chandra and XMM.

- **X-ray sources** are stars and galaxies that give out X-rays.

- **The first and brightest X-ray source** found (apart from the Sun) was the star Scorpius X-1 in 1962. Now tens of thousands are known, although most are weak.

- **Remnants of supernovae,** such as the Crab nebula, are strong sources of X-ray.

- **The strongest sources of X-ray** in the Milky Way are X-ray binaries such as Scorpius X-1 and Cygnus X-1 (see binary stars). Some are thought to contain black holes.

- **X-ray binaries** pump out 1000 trillion times as much X-ray radiation as the Sun.

- **Outside the Milky Way**, X-ray galaxies harbouring big black holes are powerful X-ray sources.

▶ *The Sun was the first X-ray source to be discovered.*

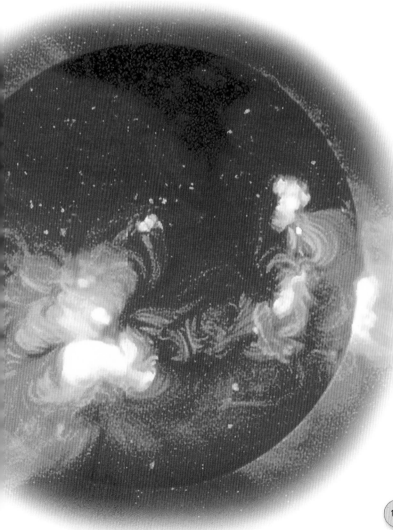

Cosmic rays

▼ *In gas clouds left by supernovae, such as the Crab Nebula, cosmic rays speed up. They give out a kind of radiation called synchrotron radiation, which can be picked up by radio telescopes.*

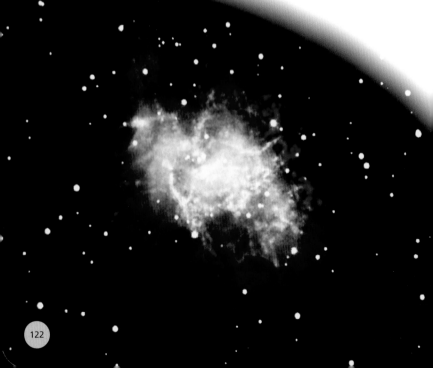

- **Streams of high-energy particles** that strike the Earth's atmosphere are called cosmic rays.

- **The lowest-energy cosmic rays** come from the Sun, or are Galactic Cosmic Rays from outside the Solar System.

- **Medium-energy cosmic rays** come from sources within the Milky Way, including powerful supernovae explosions.

- **The highest-energy cosmic rays** may come from outside the Milky Way.

- **About 90 percent of GCRs** are the nuclei of hydrogen atoms stripped of their electron (see atoms).

- **Most other GCRs** are helium and heavier nuclei, but there are also tiny positrons, electrons and neutrinos.

- **Neutrinos are so small** that they pass almost straight through the Earth without stopping.

- **The study of cosmic rays** provided scientists with most of their early knowledge about high-energy particles. These particles can only be made on Earth in huge machines called particle accelerators.

- **Most cosmic rays** are deflected (pushed aside) by the Earth's magnetic field or collide with particles in the atmosphere long before they reach the ground.

Gravity

🪐 **The attraction, or pulling force**, between all matter is gravity.

🪐 **Gravity is what holds everything on Earth** on the ground and stops it flying off into space. It holds the Earth together, keeps the Moon orbiting the Earth, and the Earth and all the planets orbiting the Sun.

🪐 **Stars burn by squeezing** their matter together. This is caused by gravity.

🪐 **Gravity acts on all matter** in the Universe.

🪐 **The force of gravity** depends on mass (the amount of matter in an object) and distance.

🪐 **The more mass an object has**, and the closer it is to another object, the more strongly its gravity pulls.

🪐 **Black holes have the strongest** gravitational pull in the Universe.

🪐 **The basic laws of gravity** can be used for anything, including detecting an unseen planet by studying the flickers in another star's light.

🪐 **Einstein's theory of general relativity** shows that gravity not only pulls on matter, but also bends space and even time itself (see Einstein).

🪐 **Orbits are the result** of a perfect balance between the force of gravity on an object (which pulls it inward towards whatever it is orbiting) and its forward momentum (which keeps it flying straight onwards).

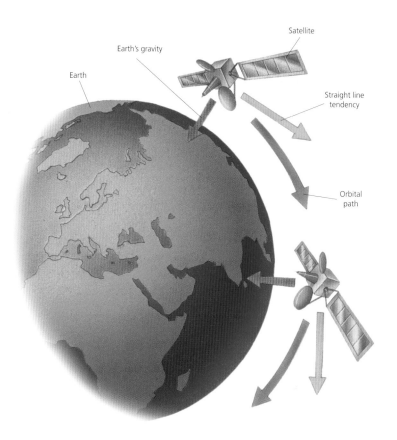

Satellite

Earth's gravity

Earth

Straight line
tendency

Orbital
path

▲ Newton showed that an object will move in a straight line at a constant speed, unless a force acts on it. The force of Earth's gravity pulls on a satellite, resulting in a curved path, or orbit.

Dark matter

🪐 **Space matter that cannot be seen** is called dark matter. Unlike stars and galaxies, it does not give off light.

🪐 **There is much more dark matter** in the Universe than bright. Some scientists think 97 percent of matter is dark.

🪐 **Astronomers know about dark matter** because its gravity pulls on stars and galaxies, changing their orbits and the way they rotate (spin round).

🪐 **The visible stars in the Milky Way** galaxy are only a thin part, embedded in a big ball of dark matter.

🪐 **Dark matter is of two kinds** – the matter in galaxies (galactic) and the matter between them (intergalactic).

🪐 **Galactic dark matter** may be similar to ordinary matter. However, it burnt out early in the life of the Universe.

🪐 **Intergalactic dark matter** is made up of WIMPs (Weakly Interacting Massive Particles).

🪐 **Some WIMPs are called cold, dark matter** because they are travelling slowly.

🪐 **Other WIMPs are called hot, dark matter** because they are travelling very quickly.

🪐 **The future of the Universe** may depend on how much dark matter there is. If there is too much, its gravity will eventually stop the Universe's expansion, and make it shrink again (see Big Bang).

▼ *A galaxy's bright stars may be only a tiny part of its total matter. Much of the galaxy may be invisible dark matter.*

Neutrinos

🪐 **Neutrinos are electrically neutral** sub-atomic particles that are produced in great numbers by the nuclear reactions that take place inside stars.

🪐 **Neutrinos travel through space** at the speed of light in straight lines, and are only affected by the weak nuclear force and gravity.

▼ *The Super Kamiokande is a joint US-Japanese project to build the world's largest underground neutrino detector.*

- **Neutrinos interact very weakly** with matter, and countless trillions of neutrinos travel straight through the Earth each day.

- **Once thought to be 'ghost' particles** that had no mass, neutrinos do in fact have a very small mass.

- **The mass of neutrinos** was once believed to be one of the main components of dark matter, but this has since been shown to be false.

- **US astronomer R Davis Jnr**, who was awarded a Nobel Prize in 2002, was the first to detect neutrinos produced by the Sun.

- **To make his discovery**, Davis built a large steel tank deep underground and filled it with 600 tonnes of dry-cleaning fluid.

- **There are three types of neutrino** – the electron neutrino, the muon neutrino, and the tau neutrino – they sometimes change from one type to another.

- **A team of Japanese scientists**, using a tank containing 45,000 tonnes of water, were the first to observe the transformation of a muon neutrino to a tau neutrino in the late 1990s.

Atoms

- **Matter is made from small particles** called atoms. They are the building blocks of the Universe.

- **Atoms are so small** that one million could fit on the full stop at the end of this sentence.

- **Atoms are the smallest identifiable piece** of a chemical element (see elements).

- **There are as many different atoms** as there are elements.

- **Atoms are mostly empty space** with tiny subatomic particles (subatomic means 'smaller than an atom').

- **The core of an atom** is the nucleus, made of two kinds of subatomic particle – protons and neutrons.

- **Whizzing around the nucleus** are even tinier particles called electrons.

- **Electrons have a negative electrical charge**, and protons have a positive charge. Electrons are held to the nucleus by electrical attraction.

- **Under certain conditions**, atoms can be split into more than 200 kinds of short-lived subatomic particle. The particles of the nucleus are made from various tiny particles called quarks.

DID YOU KNOW?
Quarks came into existence when the Universe had existed for less than one second.

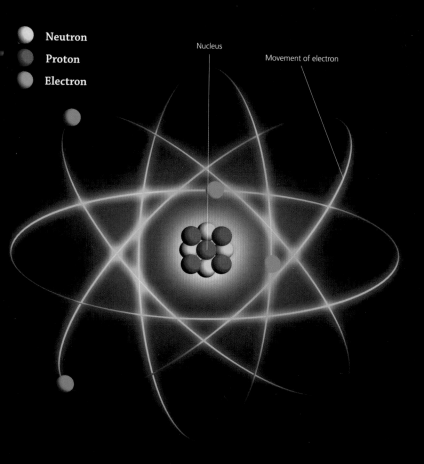

Neutron

Proton

Electron

Nucleus

Movement of electron

▲ *In the centre of the atom is the nucleus, made up of equal numbers of protons and neutrons. These are bonded by a very strong force, which can be used to create nuclear energy.*

Elements

▼ All the atoms that make up a single element have the same number of protons. All atoms except those of the simplest form of hydrogen also contain neutrons (particles with no electric charge) in their nucleus. Electrons circle the nucleus at different distances depending on how much energy they have.

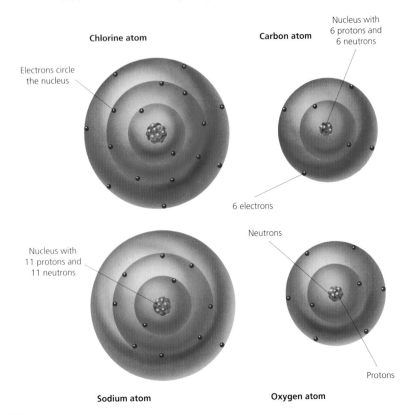

Chlorine atom

Electrons circle the nucleus

Carbon atom

Nucleus with 6 protons and 6 neutrons

6 electrons

Nucleus with 11 protons and 11 neutrons

Neutrons

Protons

Sodium atom

Oxygen atom

The basic chemicals of the Universe are elements. There are no simpler substances, and they cannot be broken down into other substances.

Elements are formed entirely of atoms that contain the same number of protons in their nuclei (see atoms). For example, all hydrogen atoms have one proton.

Hydrogen atom

Single electron

Nucleus with single proton

More than 100 elements are known.

The simplest and lightest elements, hydrogen and helium, formed very early in the history of the Universe (see Big Bang).

Other elements formed as the nuclei of the atoms of the light elements joined by nuclear fusion.

Nuclear fusion of element atoms happens deep inside stars at the end of their lives.

Lighter elements, such as oxygen and carbon, are the first to form.

Helium nuclei fuse with oxygen and neon atoms to form atoms, such as silicon, magnesium and calcium.

Heavy atoms form when supergiant stars reach the end of their life and collapse, boosting the pressure of the gravity in their core.

Periodic table

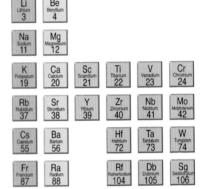

- **A logical arrangement** of all the chemical elements, the periodic table was first produced by the Russian scientist Dmitri Mendeleyev (1834–1907), and was later modified by British physicist Henry Mosely (1887–1915).

- **Elements are arranged** according to their atomic number, which is the same as the number of protons in the nucleus.

- **Although some elements** (eg Ytterbium) had yet to be discovered when Mendeleyev produced his table in 1869, he was able to predict their existence and leave appropriate gaps.

- **The horizontal rows** are called periods and contain elements that have the same number of electron shells around the nucleus.

- **There are eight** vertical columns that are called groups, and these contain elements that have similar chemical properties – such as group 0 on the far right that contains the inert noble gases.

- **Group I** contains the alkali metals – surprisingly, hydrogen is chemically an alkali metal.

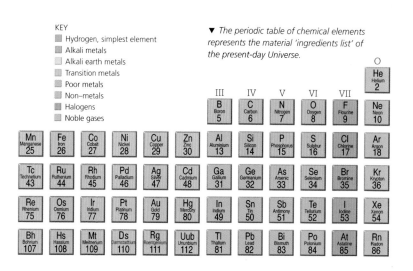

KEY
- Hydrogen, simplest element
- Alkali metals
- Alkali earth metals
- Transition metals
- Poor metals
- Non–metals
- Halogens
- Noble gases

▼ *The periodic table of chemical elements represents the material 'ingredients list' of the present-day Universe.*

🪐 **Group II** contains the alkali earth metals. Groups III to VII contain poor metals and non-metals, with the halogens in group VII.

🪐 **The metallic transition elements** (which have incomplete inner electron shells) are located in the middle between groups II and III.

🪐 **Medeleyev's original table** consisted of the 92 naturally occurring elements. Since then 19 transuranic artificial elements, made in nuclear reactors, have been added.

Life

- **Life is only known** to exist on Earth, but in 1996, NASA found what they thought might be fossils of microscopic living things in a rock from Mars.

- **Life on Earth** probably began 3.8 billion years ago.

- **The first life forms** were probably bacteria that lived in very hot water around underwater volcanoes.

- **Most scientists believe** that life's basic chemicals formed on Earth. Others think that they came from space, maybe on comets.

- **Basic organic chemicals**, such as amino acids, have been detected in nebulae and meteorites (see meteors).

- **Huge lightning flashes** may have caused big organic molecules to form on the Earth when it was young.

- **Earth is suitable for life** because of its gas atmosphere, surface water and moderately warm temperatures.

- **Saturn's icy moon**, Titan, has evidence of organic (life) chemicals in its atmosphere.

- **Jupiter's moon, Europa**, probably has water below its surface, which could spawn life.

▶ The surface of Mars – the only other planet that once had water on its surface.

▲ *This artist's impression shows the Huygens probe plunging through the clouds in Titan's atmosphere, gathering information as it descends.*

DID YOU KNOW?

On Earth, life exists everywhere in all conditions – hot, cold, wet and dry. However, no signs of life have been found anywhere else.

Extraterrestrials

🪐 **Extraterrestrial (ET) means** 'outside the Earth'.

🪐 **Some scientists believe** that ET life could develop anywhere in the Universe where there is a flow of energy.

🪐 **Most scientists believe** that if there is ET life anywhere else in the Universe, it is probably based on the chemistry of carbon, as life on Earth is.

▼ *People have reported spotting UFOs (Unidentified Flying Objects), sometimes called flying saucers, for more than 60 years.*

- **If civilizations exist** elsewhere, they may be on planets circling other stars.

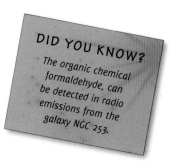

DID YOU KNOW?
The organic chemical formaldehyde, can be detected in radio emissions from the galaxy NGC 253.

- **The Drake Equation** was proposed by astronomer Frank Drake to calculate how many civilizations there could be in our galaxy – the figure is millions.

- **There is no proof** that any ET life form has ever visited Earth.

- **Search for Extraterrestrial Intelligence (SETI)** is a program that analyzes radio signals from space for signs of intelligent life.

- **The Arecibo radio telescope** beamed out a signal to distant stars to try to communicate with extraterrestrial life.

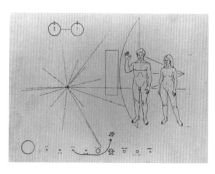

◀ The space probes Pioneer 10 and 11 carry metal panels with picture messages about life on Earth into deep space.

Stars and galaxies

Stars

🪐 **Stars are balls of gas**, mainly hydrogen and helium.

🪐 **Nuclear reactions in the heart of stars**, such as those in nuclear bombs, generate enormous energy, which the stars send out as heat and light.

🪐 **The heart of a star** reaches 16 million°C. A grain of sand this hot could kill someone 150 km away.

🪐 **The gas in stars** is in a special hot state called plasma, which is made of atoms stripped of electrons.

🪐 **In the core of a star**, hydrogen nuclei fuse (join together) to form helium. This nuclear reaction is called a proton-proton chain.

Large white star

Medium-sized star

Small red star

▲ *Large stars are hot and white, and smaller stars are cool and red. A large star can make energy faster and get much hotter than a smaller star. Medium-sized stars, such as our Sun, look yellow.*

🪐 **Stars twinkle** because they are seen through the Earth's atmosphere.

🪐 **Astronomers work out the size of a star** from its brightness and its temperature.

🪐 **The size and brightness** of a star depends on its mass – how much gas it is made of. The Sun is a medium-sized star. No star has more than 100 times the Sun's mass or less than 6–7 percent of its mass.

🪐 **The coolest stars**, such as Arcturus and Antares, glow reddest. Hotter stars are yellow and white. The hottest are blue-white, like Rigel and Zeta Puppis.

🪐 **The blue supergiant, Zeta Puppis**, has a surface temperature of 40,000°C, while Rigel's is 10,000°C.

▶ A swarm, or large cluster of stars known as M80 (NGC 6093), from the Milky Way. This swarm, 28,000 light years from Earth, contains hundreds of thousands of stars, 'attracted' to each other by gravity.

Star birth

🪐 **Medium-sized stars** last for about ten billion years. Small stars may last for 200 billion years.

🪐 **Big stars have short, fierce lives** of ten million years.

🪐 **Stars that begin life** in clouds of gas and dust are called nebulae.

🪐 **Inside nebulae**, gravity creates dark clumps called EGGs (evaporating gaseous globules). Each clump contains the seeds of a family of stars.

🪐 **As gravity squeezes** these globules, they shrink and form hot balls of gas and dust.

🪐 **Smaller clumps** don't get very hot, so they eventually fizzle out.

🪐 **If a larger clump** reaches 10 million°C in its core, hydrogen atoms begin to join together in nuclear reactions and the baby star starts to glow.

🪐 **In a medium-sized star**, such as the Sun, the heat of burning hydrogen pushes gas out as fiercely as gravity pulls inwards, and the star becomes stable (steady).

◀ *In the centre of this massive galactic nebula is a cluster of young, bright stars.*

▼ *Stars are born and die all over the Universe, and by looking at stars in different stages of their life, astronomers have learned about the stages of their existence.*

1 Clumps of gas in a nebula start to shrink into tight balls that will become stars

2 The gas spirals as it is pulled inwards. Any leftover gas and dust may form planets around the new star

3 Deep in its centre, the new star starts making energy, but it is still hidden by the cloud of dust and gas

4 The dust and gas are blown away and the shining star can be seen

Small stars

🪐 **Depending on their colour**, small stars of low brightness are called white, red or black dwarves.

🪐 **Red dwarves are bigger** than the planet Jupiter, but smaller than the medium-sized star, the Sun. They glow faintly with less than 5 percent of the Sun's brightness.

🪐 **No red dwarf can be seen** with the naked eye – not even the nearest star to the Sun, the red dwarf Proxima Centauri.

🪐 **White dwarves are the last stage** in the life of a medium-sized star. Although they are even smaller than red dwarves, they contain the same amount of matter as the Sun.

🪐 **The star 40 Eridani** is really three dwarf stars – a white dwarf and a red dwarf circling a small orange star, which can just be seen with the naked eye.

🪐 **Brown dwarves** are cool space objects, a little bigger than Jupiter. They formed in the same way as other stars, but were not big enough to start shining properly. They just glow very faintly with the heat left over from their formation.

1 Pup star
2 Sirius

◀ The night sky's brightest star, Sirius the Dog Star, has a white dwarf companion called the Pup Star.

🪐 **Black dwarves** are very small, cold, dead stars. They were either not big enough to start shining, or they have burnt all their nuclear fuel and stopped glowing.

DID YOU KNOW?
The smallest kind of star is called a neutron star.

▼ *Ejecting gas outwards, this planetary nebula is the closest example of the way a star evolves into a white dwarf.*

147

Giant stars

▼ A giant star expanding and ejecting matter.

▶ *The constellation Cygnus, the Swan, contains a group of giant blue stars including one of the brightest known, almost 100 times as big as the Sun.*

🪐 **Giant stars** are 10 to 100 times as big as the Sun, and 10 to 1000 times as bright.

🪐 **Red giants are stars** that have swollen 10 to 100 times their size, as they reach the last stages of their life and their outer gas layers cool and expand.

🪐 **Giant stars have burnt** all their hydrogen, and so burn helium, fusing (joining) helium atoms to make carbon.

🪐 **The biggest stars** continue to swell after they become red giants. They then grow into supergiants.

🪐 **Supergiant stars are up to 500 times** as big as the Sun, with absolute magnitudes of −5 to −10 (see star brightness).

🪐 **Pressure in the heart** of a supergiant is enough to fuse carbon atoms together to make iron.

🪐 **All the iron in the Universe** was made in the hearts of supergiant stars.

🪐 **There is a limit to the brightness** of supergiants, so they can be used as distance markers by comparing how bright they look to how bright they are (see distances).

🪐 **Supergiant stars** eventually collapse and explode as supernovae.

149

Star brightness

🪐 **Star brightness is measured** on a scale of magnitude that was first devised in 150 BC by the ancient Greek astronomer Hipparchus.

🪐 **The brightest star** that Hipparchus could see was Antares, and he described it as magnitude 1. He described the faintest star he could see as magnitude 6.

🪐 **Using telescopes and binoculars**, astronomers can now see much fainter stars than Hipparchus could.

🪐 **Good binoculars show** magnitude 9 stars, while a home telescope will show magnitude 10 stars.

🪐 **Brighter stars than Antares** have been identified with magnitudes of less than 1, and even minus numbers. Betelgeuse is 0.5, Vega is 0.03, and the Sun is –26.7.

🪐 **After the Sun**, the brightest star visible from Earth is Sirius, the Dog Star, with a magnitude of –1.46.

🪐 **The magnitude scale only describes** how bright a star looks from Earth compared to other stars. This is its relative magnitude.

🪐 **The further away a star is**, the dimmer it looks and the smaller its relative magnitude is, regardless of how bright it really is.

🪐 **A star's absolute magnitude** describes how bright a star actually is.

🪐 **The star Deneb** is 60,000 times brighter than the Sun. However, as it is about 1800 light years away, it looks dimmer than Sirius.

▲ To estimate a star's magnitude, its brightness is compared to two stars with known magnitude – one star a little brighter and one a little dimmer.

H-R diagram

🌀 **Devised by Ejnar Hertzsprung and Henry Russell**, the Hertzsprung-Russell (H-R) diagram is a graph to plot the temperature of stars against their brightness. The temperature of a star is indicated by its colour.

🌀 **Cool stars are red** or reddish-yellow.

🌀 **Hot stars burn** white or blue.

🌀 **Medium-sized stars** form a diagonal band called the main sequence across the graph.

🌀 **The whiter and hotter a main sequence star is**, the brighter it shines. White stars and blue-white stars are usually bigger and younger.

🌀 **The redder and cooler a star is**, the dimmer it glows. Cool red stars tend to be smaller and older.

🌀 **Giant stars and white dwarf stars** lie to either side of the main sequence stars.

🌀 **The H-R diagram shows** how bright each colour star should be. If the star actually looks dimmer, it must be further away.

> **DID YOU KNOW?**
> The H-R diagram shows the temperature and brightness of different types of stars.

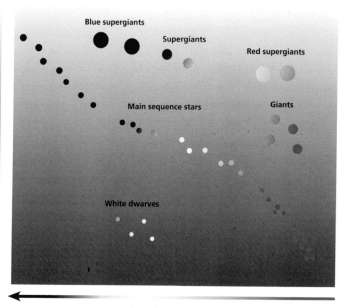

Blue supergiants

Supergiants

Red supergiants

Main sequence stars

Giants

White dwarves

Increasing brightness

Increasing temperature

▲ *By comparing a star's brightness, predicted by the H-R diagram, with how bright it really looks, astronomers can work out how far away it is.*

Binary stars

- **The Sun is alone in space**, but most stars are in groups of two or more.

- **Binaries are double stars** and there are various kinds.

- **True binary stars are two stars** that are held together by one another's gravity.

- **Optical binaries** are not binaries at all. They are two stars that look as if they are together because they are in roughly the same line of sight from the Earth.

- **Eclipsing binaries are true binary stars** that spin around in exactly the same line of sight from the Earth, and keep blocking out each other's light.

- **Spectroscopic binaries are true binaries** that spin so closely together that the only way of knowing that there are two stars is by the changes in colour.

- **The star Epsilon**, in the constellation of Lyra, is called the Double Double because it is a pair of binaries.

- **Mizar, in Ursa Major**, was the first binary star to be discovered by telescope in about 1617.

- **Mizar and its companion**, Alcor, form an optical binary.

- **Albireo, in Cygnus**, is an optical binary that is visible to the naked eye – one star looks gold in colour and the other looks blue.

Two similar stars follow each other in circular orbit

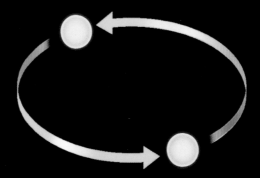

A smaller star orbits a large star

▲ *Many stars are binaries or multiples – two or more stars close together. Their motions depend on their sizes.*

Variable stars

🌀 **Variable stars are stars** that do not burn steadily like the Sun, but flare up and down.

🌀 **Pulsating variables are stars** that expand and contract. They include stars known as Cepheid variables and RR Lyrae variables.

🌀 **Cepheid variables are big**, bright stars that pulsate with energy, flaring up regularly every one to 50 days.

🌀 **Cepheid variables are so predictable** in brightness that they make good distance markers (see distances).

🌀 **RR Lyrae variables are yellow** supergiant stars near the end of their life that flicker as their fuel runs down.

▼ The spiral galaxy NGC 4603 – the most distant galaxy in which Cepheid variables have been discovered.

► *The constellation of Cygnus contains a vanishing star.*

🪐 **Mira-type variables** are similar to Mira in Cetus, the Whale, and vary regularly over months or years.

🪐 **RV Tauri variables** are very unpredictable, flaring up and down over changing periods of time.

🪐 **Eclipsing variables** are really eclipsing binaries (see binary stars). They seem to flare up and down, but in fact are simply one star getting in the way of the other.

🪐 **The Demon Star** is Algol in Perseus. It seems to burn fiercely for 59 hours, become dim, then flare up again ten hours later. It is really an eclipsing binary.

🪐 **The vanishing star** is Chi in Cygnus, the Swan. It can be seen with the naked eye for a few months each year, but then becomes so dim that it cannot be seen, even with large amateur telescopes.

Novae

- **A nova** (plural novas or novae), which means 'new' in Latin, was the name given by early astronomers to the temporary appearance of a bright star in the sky.

- **In fact, a nova is a star** that suddenly becomes up to a million times brighter than normal and then fades back to its original luminosity.

- **For a few weeks in 1901** the nova GK Persei outshone every other star in the sky except Sirius.

- **Some novas appear to fade** within a few days, while others may take more than one year to return to their former dim state.

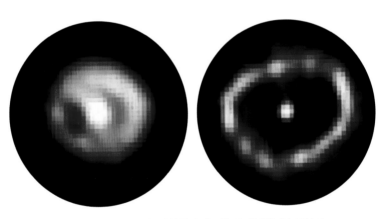

▲ Two views of the nova Cygni 1992 obtained by the Hubble Faint Object Camera. The image on the right has been processed to reveal the shell of hot gas surrounding the 'parent' star.

🌑 **Novas are produced** by binary stars where one of the pair is a white dwarf and the other is a larger and cooler star.

DID YOU KNOW?

The material ejected by a nova can travel through space at speeds up to 1500 km per hour.

🌑 **The white dwarf's gravity** pulls hydrogen and other stellar material away from its companion star and this material builds up in layers around the surface of the white dwarf.

🌑 **As more material accumulates**, the temperature in the lowest layer steadily increases until it reaches about 20 million degrees, at which point the hydrogen ignites into a massive nuclear explosion.

🌑 **This explosion** blows away the upper layers of material in an expanding spherical cloud of glowing hot gas, and the process starts all over again.

🌑 **Novae that have only** been observed to flare up once are known as classical novae, while those that have been seen on more than one occasion are known as recurrent novae.

Supernovae

- **A supernova** is the final, gigantic explosion of a supergiant star at the end of its life.

- **A supernova lasts** for just a week or so, but shines as brightly as a galaxy of 100 billion ordinary stars.

- **Supernovae occur when a supergiant star** uses up its hydrogen and helium fuel and shrinks. This boosts pressure in its core, enough to fuse heavy elements such as iron (see nuclear energy).

- **When iron begins to fuse** in its core, a star collapses instantly – then rebounds in a mighty explosion.

- **Seen in 1987, supernova 1987A** was the first viewed with the naked eye since Kepler's 1604 sighting.

- **Supernova remnants** (leftovers) are the gigantic, cloudy shells of material swelling out from supernovae.

- **A supernova seen by Chinese** astronomers in AD 185 was thought to be such a bad omen that it sparked a revolution.

- **A dramatic supernova** was seen by Chinese astronomers in 1054, creating the Crab nebula.

- **Elements heavier** than iron are made in supernovae.

DID YOU KNOW?
Many of the elements that make up the human body were forged in supernovae.

▶ A supernova looks like a bright new star. The last one seen in the Milky Way was more than 400 years ago.

Neutron stars

- **Mainly made up of neutrons** (see atoms), neutron stars are incredibly small, super-dense stars with a solid crust made of iron and similar elements.

- **Although neutron stars** weigh as much as the Sun, they are just 20 km across on average.

- **A tablespoon of neutron star** would weigh about one million tonnes.

- **Neutron stars form** from the central core of a star that has died in a supernova explosion.

- **To produce a neutron star**, a star must be more than 1.4 times as massive as a medium-sized star, such as the Sun. This is the Chandrasekhar limit.

- **A star more than three times** as massive as the Sun would collapse beyond a neutron star to form a black hole. This is called the Oppenheimer-Volkoff limit.

- **The first evidence** of neutron stars came when pulsars were discovered in the 1960s.

- **Some stars giving out X-rays**, such as Hercules X-1, are neutron stars. The X-rays come from nearby stars as material is squeezed on to their surfaces by their gravity.

- **Neutron stars have very powerful magnetic fields**, billions of times stronger than the Earth's, which stretch the atoms out into frizzy 'whiskers' on the star's surface.

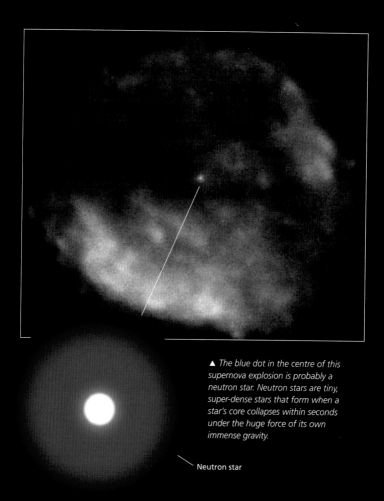

▲ The blue dot in the centre of this supernova explosion is probably a neutron star. Neutron stars are tiny, super-dense stars that form when a star's core collapses within seconds under the huge force of its own immense gravity.

Neutron star

163

Pulsars

- **A pulsar is a neutron star** that spins rapidly, beaming out regular pulses of radio waves.

- **The first pulsar** was detected by Cambridge astronomer, Jocelyn Bell Burnell, in 1967.

- **At first, astronomers thought** the regular pulses might be signals from aliens, and pulsars were jokingly called LGMs (Little Green Men).

- **Most pulsars send** their radio pulse about once a second. The slowest pulse only every eight seconds, and the fastest every 1.4 milliseconds.

- **As it gets older**, the pulse rate of a pulsar slows down.

- **The Crab pulsar** slows by a millionth of a second a day.

- **More than 1500 pulsars** are now known, but there may be 100,000 active in the Milky Way.

- **Pulsars probably result** from a supernova explosion – that is why most are found in the flat disc of the Milky Way, where supernovae occur.

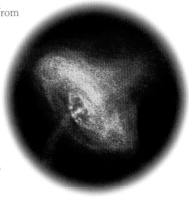

▶ The Crab Nebula is the remnants of a stellar explosion. In this image, taken by the Chandra X-Ray Observatory, the central pulsar is clearly shown.

▲ *A pulsar, discovered in 1992, which has three planets circling it. The pulsar's magnetic fields are shown as a blue glow.*

Pulsars are not found in the same place as supernovae because they form after the debris from the explosion has spread into space.

With such rapid pulses, pulsars must be tiny neutron stars – anything larger could not spin as fast.

Stellar clusters

🌀 **A stellar cluster** is a group of stars (a stellar system) where the constituent stars are located much more closely together than the surrounding stars.

🌀 **There are two distinct types of stellar cluster** – open clusters and globular clusters.

▼ A telescope reveals that the Pleiades cluster contains many more stars than the bright stars that have given it the popular name 'Seven Sisters'.

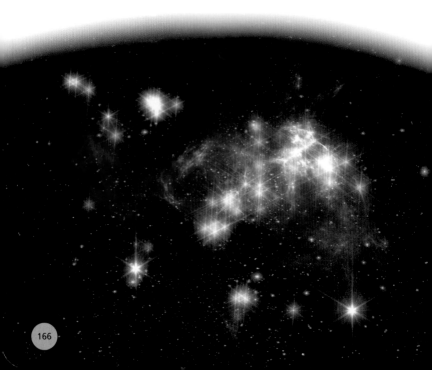

- **Open clusters contain** between a few hundred and several thousand fairly young stars, and they are mainly located in the same plane (ecliptic) as the spiral arms of the galaxy.

- **Most open clusters** are less than 200 million years old, and in some clusters the stars are so young (only a few million years old) that they are still embedded in the clouds from which they emerged.

- **The most famous** open cluster is the Pleiades, which is also known as the Seven Sisters – although there are nine stars in the cluster that are visible to the unaided eye.

- **Globular clusters are much bigger** than open clusters and contain up to one million stars. They are also much older, with an average age of at least 10 billion years.

- **The globular cluster M92** has an estimated age of 13–14 billion years, making it almost as old as the Universe itself.

- **In our galaxy**, the globular clusters are mainly located above and below the galactic plane, and they are concentrated around the centre in a spherical cloud that is called the galactic halo.

- **Stars in globular clusters** are sometimes described as metal-poor because they were formed so long ago, before the Universe contained many metal atoms.

- **Younger stars**, like our Sun and the stars in open clusters, are considered to be metal-rich.

Nebulae

🌀 **Any fuzzy patch of light** in the night sky was once called a nebula. Nowadays, many of these are known to be galaxies.

🌀 **Nebulae are gigantic clouds** of gas and space dust.

🌀 **Glowing nebulae** give off a dim, red light as the hydrogen gas in them is heated by radiation from nearby stars.

🌀 **The Orion Nebula** is a glowing nebula just visible to the naked eye.

🌀 **Reflection nebulae** have no light. They can only be seen because starlight shines off the dust in them.

🌀 **Dark nebulae not only have no light** of their own, they also soak up all light. They can only be seen as patches of darkness, blocking out light from the stars behind them.

🌀 **The Horsehead Nebula in Orion** is the best known dark nebula. As its name suggests, it is shaped like a horse's head.

🌀 **Planetary nebulae** are thin rings of gas cloud that are thrown out by dying stars. Despite their name, they have nothing to do with planets.

🌀 **The Ring Nebula in Lyra** is the best known of the planetary nebulae.

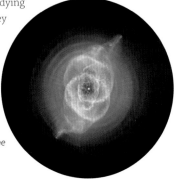

▶ One of the most complex nebulae to be discovered is the Cat's Eye Nebula (NGC 6543).

▶ The Trifid Nebula glows as hydrogen and helium gas within is heated by radiation from stars.

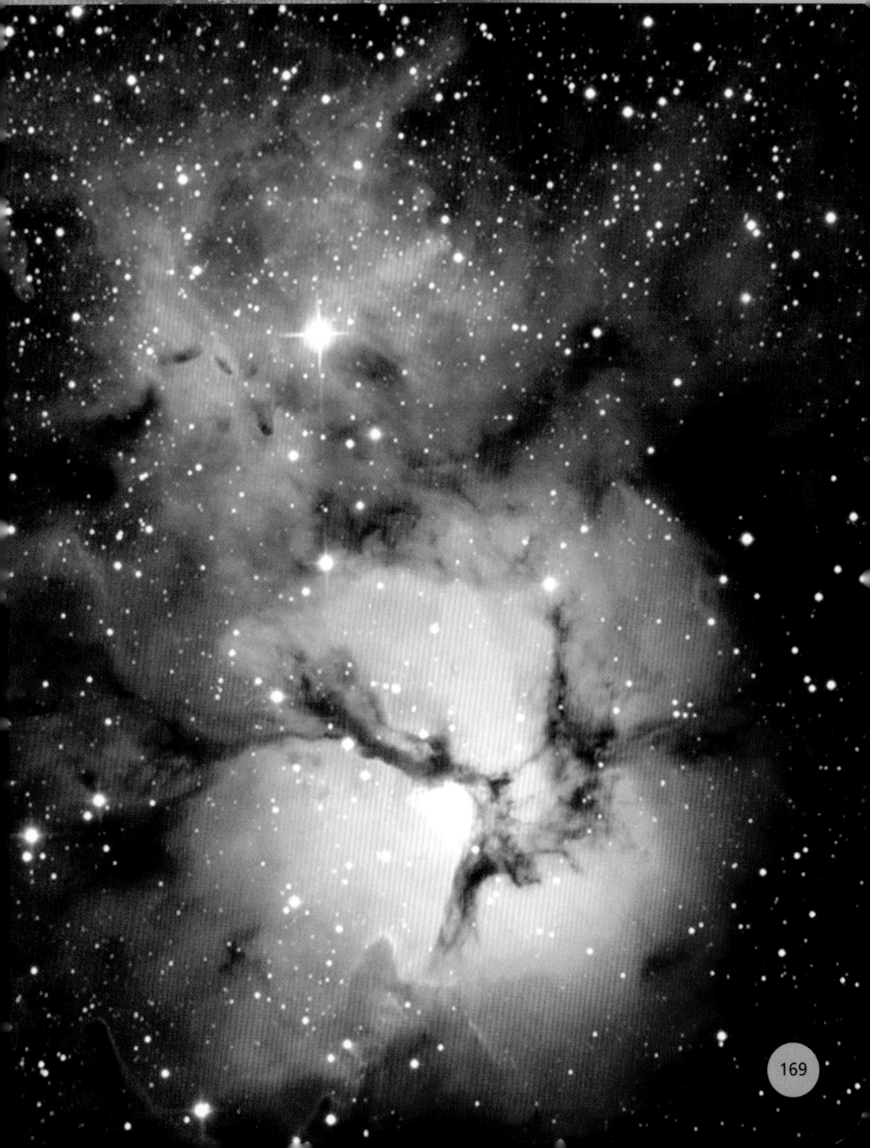

Black holes

- **Gravity is so strong** in black holes that it sucks everything in, including light.

- **If a human fell** into a black hole, they would stretch like spaghetti.

🪐 **When a star or galaxy** becomes so dense that it collapses under the pull of its own gravity, black holes are created.

🪐 **Black holes** may exist at the heart of every galaxy.

🪐 **Gravity shrinks** a black hole to an unimaginably small point called a singularity.

🪐 **Around a singularity**, gravity is so intense that space-time is bent into a funnel.

🪐 **Matter spiralling into a black hole** is torn apart and glows so brightly that it creates the brightest objects in the Universe – quasars.

🪐 **The swirling gases** around a black hole turn it into an electrical generator, spouting jets containing electrons that are billions of kilometres out into space.

🪐 **The opposite of black holes** may be white holes, which spray out matter and light like fountains.

🪐 **Black holes and white holes** may join to form tunnels called wormholes.

◀ *The gravity of a black hole is so strong that nothing can escape, not even light. Planets, stars, gas and dust are pulled into the hole.*

Quasars

🌀 **The most intense sources** of light in the Universe, quasars are no bigger than the Solar System, but they glow with the brightness of 100 galaxies.

🌀 **Quasars are the most distant** known objects in the Universe. Even the nearest is a billion light years away.

🌀 **The most distant quasar** is on the very edge of the known Universe, 13 billion light years away.

🌀 **Some quasars are so far away** that we see them as they were when the Universe was still in its infancy – less than 10 percent of its current age.

🌀 **Quasar is short for** Quasi-Stellar (starlike) Radio Source. This comes from the fact that the first quasars were detected by the strong radio signals they give out, and also because quasars are so small and bright that at first people thought they looked like stars.

🌀 **Less than 10 percent of the 100,000 quasars** now known actually beam out radio signals.

🌀 **The brightest quasar**, 3C 273, is 2.5 billion light years away.

🌀 **Quasars are at the heart** of some galaxies called 'active galaxies'.

🌀 **The energy used by quasars comes** from a black hole at their core, which draws in matter ferociously.

🌀 **The black hole in a quasar** may have the same mass as 100 million Suns.

▲ *This artist's impression depicts an active quasar. Winds in the outer regions of the quasar contain dust particles.*

Galaxies

🌀 **Giant groups of millions** or even trillions of stars are called galaxies. Our own local galaxy is the Milky Way.

🌀 **There may be 500 billion** galaxies in the Universe.

🌀 **Only three galaxies** are visible to the naked eye from Earth besides the Milky Way – the Large and Small Magellanic clouds, and the Andromeda Galaxy.

🌀 **In 1923**, astronomers realized that galaxies are huge star groups.

🌀 **Galaxies are often found** in groups called clusters. One cluster may contain hundreds of galaxies.

Spiral   Irregular

▲ *There are various types of galaxy in the Universe. Although they are vast, they are so far away that they look like fuzzy clouds.*

- **Spiral galaxies** are spinning galaxies with a dense core and spiralling arms.

- **Irregular galaxies** have no obvious shape. They may have formed from the debris of galaxies that crashed into each other.

- **Elliptical galaxies are vast**, old, egg-shaped galaxies, made up of as many as a trillion stars.

- **Barred spiral galaxies** have just two arms. These are linked across the middle of the galaxy by a bar from which they trail.

Elliptical   Spiral with a bar through the middle

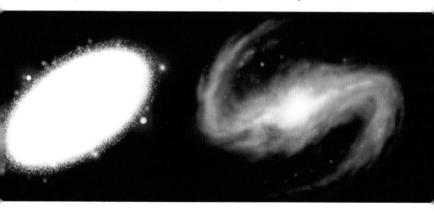

Our galaxy

- **The faint, hazy band** of light that can be seen stretching right across the night sky is the Milky Way.

- **With binoculars**, the countless stars that make up the Milky Way can be seen.

- **The Milky Way** is the view of our Galaxy from Earth.

- **This galaxy** is one of billions in space.

- **The galaxy is 100,000 light years** across and 1000 light years thick. It is made up of 100 billion stars.

- **All the stars are arranged** in a spiral with a bulge in the middle.

- **The Sun is just one** of the billions of stars on one arm of the spiral.

- **The Milky Way is whirling rapidly**, spinning the Sun and other stars around at 800,000 km/h.

- **Once every 220 million years**, the Sun travels around the Milky Way – a journey of 170,000 light years.

- **The huge bulge at the centre** of the galaxy is about 20,000 light years across and 3000 light years thick. It only contains very old stars and little dust or gas.

- **There may be a huge black hole** in the very middle of the Milky Way.

▶ *The arms at the edge of the Milky Way contain many young, bright stars, while the middle is dust and gas.*

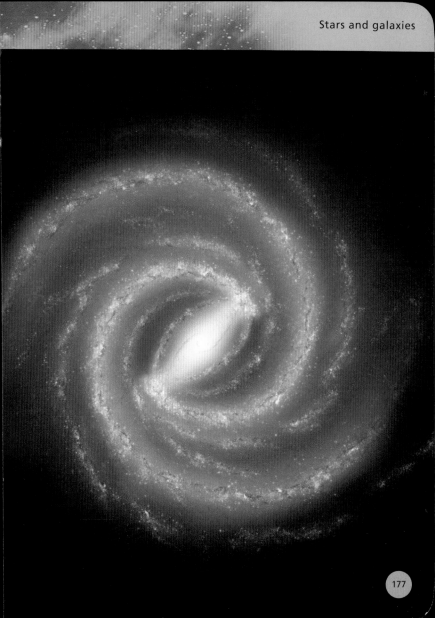

Local group

- **In 1936**, the term Local Group was coined by Edwin Hubble to describe the cluster of nearby galaxies to which the Milky Way galaxy belongs.

- **There are 43 galaxies** now identified as belonging to the Local group, more than half of which have only been discovered during the last 30 years. All of the galaxies in the Local Group interact gravitationally.

- **In addition to the Milky Way**, there are two other spiral galaxies in the Local Group, the Andromeda Galaxy (M31) and the smaller M33. Our galaxy and M31 together contain over 99 percent of the mass of the Local Group.

- **All of the other members of the Local group** are dwarf galaxies, of which the best known are the Large Magellanic Cloud and the Small Magellanic Cloud.

- **Some of the dwarf galaxies** are so dim that their brightness is less than that of the night sky, making them difficult to detect.

- **The Milky Way has 13 dwarf galaxies** that orbit around it in the same way that moons orbit around a planet.

- **The Sagittarius dwarf galaxy** is so close that it is in the process of being absorbed into the Milky Way.

- **The Local Group** is also interacting with nearby groups of galaxies. It has stretched the Sculptor Group so much that there is no gap of intergalactic space between them.

- **On an even larger scale**, the Local Group is slowing falling towards the nearby Virgo Cluster of galaxies.

▲ The Large Magellanic Cloud is located 157,000 light years from the Earth. It is affected by the gravity of our Milky Way galaxy and in turn its gravitational force is distorting its close neighbour, the Small Magellanic Cloud.

Star names

Most of the brightest stars in the night sky were given individual names by the ancient Greeks. Arabic-speaking astronomers renamed many of these during the Middle Ages.

▼ *Canis Major (Great Dog) is a rare example of a constellation name being derived from a particular star – in this case Sirius, which has long been known as the 'Dog Star'.*

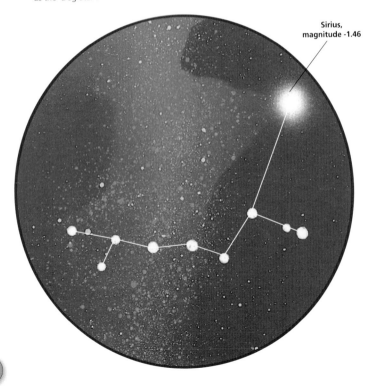

Sirius,
magnitude -1.46

- **Arcturus means 'bear warden'** in Greek, and the star was given that name because it appears to follow the Great Bear across the sky.

- **The star Beta Orionis** was named Rigel (which means 'the foot' in Arabic) because it forms one of the hunter's feet in the constellation of Orion.

- **Alpha Orionis has the name Betelgeuse** (pronounced 'beetle-juice'), which is meaningless. The original Arabic name was Yad al-Jawza (which means 'the hand of Orion').

- **The constellation of Libra** was once known as the Scorpion's Claws. Consequently, the two brightest stars are Zubenelchemale ('Northern Claw') and Zubenelgenubi ('Southern Claw').

- **In 1603**, the German astronomer Johan Bayer introduced the present system of designating the brightest stars in a constellation by the letters of the Greek alphabet.

- **Variable stars have their own system**. They are designated by constellation in order of discovery in the sequence R, S, T, U, V, W, X, Y, Z. After Z the next variable star in the constellation is designated RR, and the next RS and so on.

- **England's first Astronomer Royal**, John Flamsteed (1646–1719), preferred a different system in which all the visible stars in a constellation were given a number. Some stars, such as 61 Cygni, are still known by their Flamsteed numbers.

Star patterns

▼ *Despite the large number of stars captured in this image, the constellation of Orion, the Hunter, is easy to find. It has a line of three stars in the centre called Orion's belt (see middle right).*

- **Patterns of stars in the sky** are called constellations. Astronomers use them to pinpoint individual stars.

- **Most of the constellations** were identified long ago by the stargazers of ancient Babylon and Greece.

- **Constellations are simply patterns** – there is no real link between the stars.

- **Astronomers today recognize** 88 constellations (see pp276–365).

- **Heroes and creatures of Greek myth,** such as Orion and Perseus, provided the names for many constellations, although each name is usually written in its Latin form, not in Greek.

- **The stars in each constellation** are named after a letter of the Greek alphabet.

- **The brightest star in each constellation** is called the Alpha star, the next brightest Beta, and so on.

- **Different constellations** become visible at different times of year, as the Earth travels around the Sun.

- **Southern Hemisphere constellations** are different from those in the north.

- **The constellation of the Great Bear,** also known by its Latin name Ursa Major, contains an easily recognizable group of seven stars called the Plough or the Big Dipper.

Celestial sphere

🐚 **Stars seem to move across** the sky as though they are on the inside of a giant ball. This is the celestial sphere.

🐚 **The northern tip** is called the North Celestial Pole. The southern tip is the South Celestial Pole.

🐚 **The celestial sphere appears to rotate** on an axis that runs between its two celestial poles.

🐚 **There is an equator** around the middle of the celestial sphere, just like Earth's.

🐚 **The positions of the stars** on the celestial sphere are given by their declination (Dec.) and right ascension (R.A.).

🐚 **Declination is like latitude**. It is measured in degrees and shows a star's position between the pole and the equator.

🐚 **Right ascension is like longitude**. It is measured in hours, minutes and seconds, and shows how far a star is from the First Point of Aries.

🐚 **The zenith** is the point on the sphere above a person's head as they look into the night sky.

E

Scorp

▶ The celestial sphere is like a great blue ball dotted with stars, with the Earth in the middle. Its boundaries are imaginary, but the concept makes it easy to locate stars and constellations. The zodiac is shown on the inset.

| **1** Northern tip |
| **2** Southern tip |
| **3** Declination line |
| **4** Right ascension line (First point of Aries) |

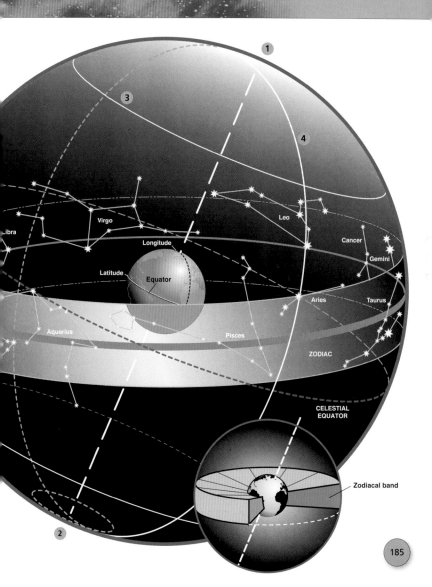

Virgo

Libra

Leo

Cancer

Gemini

Longitude

Latitude

Equator

Aries

Taurus

Aquarius

Pisces

ZODIAC

CELESTIAL
EQUATOR

Zodiacal band

Star charts

🪐 **Plotting the positions** of the stars in the sky is complex because there are a vast number of them and because they are at hugely different distances.

🪐 **The first modern star charts** were the German Bonner Durchmusterung (BD) charts of 1863, which show the positions of 324,189 stars. The German word Durchmusterung means 'scanning through'.

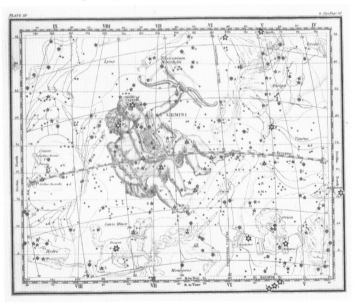

▲ A section of an old star chart showing the constellation of Gemini.

🪐 **Published 1890 to 1945,** the AGK1 chart of the German Astronomical Society showed 200,000 stars.

🪐 **The AGK charts** are now on version AGK3 and remain the standard star chart. They are compiled from photographs.

🪐 **The measurements of accurate places** for huge numbers of stars depends on the careful determination of 1535 stars in the Fundamental Catalog (FK5).

🪐 **Photometric catalogues map** the stars by magnitude (see star brightness) and colour, as well as their position.

🪐 **Photographic star atlases** do not actually plot the position of every star on paper, but include photos of them in place instead.

🪐 **Three main atlases** are popular with astronomers – *Norton's Star Atlas*, *Tirion Sky Atlas* and *Photographischer Stern-Atlas*.

🪐 **Celestial coordinates** are the figures that plot a star's position on a ball-shaped graph (see celestial sphere).

🪐 **The altazimuth system** of coordinates gives a star's position by its altitude (its angle in degrees from the horizon) and its azimuth (its angle in degrees clockwise around the horizon, starting from north).

🪐 **The ecliptic system** does the same, using the ecliptic rather than the horizon as a starting point.

🪐 **The equatorial system** depends on the celestial equator, and gives figures called right ascensions and declination, just like latitude and longitude on Earth.

The Solar System

🪐 **The Solar System** consists of the Sun and all the objects orbiting within its gravitational field and extends to the edge of the Oort Cloud.

🪐 **There are eight planets** in the Solar System – four inner rocky planets (Mercury, Venus, Earth, Mars) and four outer gas planets (Jupiter, Saturn, Uranus, Neptune).

▼ The Solar System, with part of the Sun in the foreground, showing the relative sizes of the planets, although the distances between them have been greatly compressed.

1 Mercury	**4** Mars	**7** Uranus
2 Venus	**5** Jupiter	**8** Neptune
3 Earth	**6** Saturn	

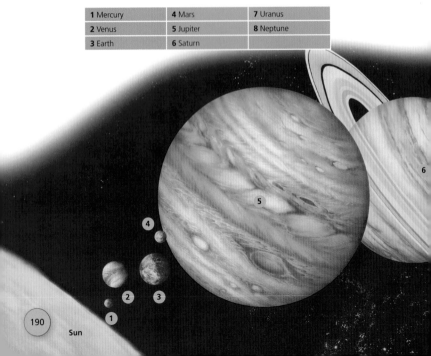

190

Sun

🪐 **The planets follow nearly circular orbits** around the Sun and they all lie in the same plane, which is known as the solar ecliptic.

🪐 **The inner and outer planets** are separated by the Asteroid Belt, which contains many thousands of asteroids. Some are more than 1000 km in diameter.

🪐 **It takes light** over four hours to travel from the Sun to Neptune.

🪐 **All the planets**, with the exception of Mercury and Venus, have at least one moon and altogether there are at least 136 moons in the Solar System.

🪐 **Pluto used to be considered a planet**, but in 2006 it was officially designated as a planetoid along with some asteroids and Kuiper Belt objects.

🪐 **The Kuiper Belt** is a disc-shaped region of space located 30–100 AU from the Sun, which contains numerous orbiting objects ranging from 50–2000 km in diameter.

🪐 **A spherical region of space** that extends between 10,000 and 200,000 AU from the Sun, the Oort Cloud contains an estimated 1000 billion comets.

🪐 **The outer edge of the Oort Cloud** (the edge of the Solar System) is about halfway to the nearest star, Alpha Centauri, which may well be surrounded by its own comet cloud.

8

7

The Sun

🌑 **This medium-sized star** measures 1,392,000 km across – 109 times the diameter of the Earth.

🌑 **Even though the Sun** is made almost entirely of hydrogen and helium, the lightest gases in the Universe, it weighs 2000 trillion trillion tonnes – about 300,000 times as much as the Earth.

🌑 **The Sun's interior** is heated by nuclear reactions to temperatures of 15 million°C.

🌑 **The visible surface layer of the Sun** is called the photosphere. This sea of boiling gas sends out the light and heat we see and feel on Earth.

🌑 **Flames called spicules** dart through a thin layer above the photosphere called the chromosphere.

🌑 **Above the chromosphere** is the Sun's halo-like corona.

🌑 **The heat from the Sun's interior** erupts on the surface in patches called granules, and gigantic arcs of hot gases called solar prominences (see solar eruptions).

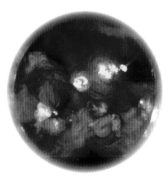

◄ This artificially coloured photo was taken by a satellite and shows the Sun's surface to be a turbulent mass of flames and tongues of hot gases – very different from the even, yellowish ball we see from Earth.

▶ Cutaway of the Sun showing its layers, and the SOHO spacecraft, which spent two years gathering information about the Sun.

| 1 Core |
| 2 Radiative zone |
| 3 Convective zone |
| 4 Photosphere |
| 5 Chromosphere |

🌑 **The Sun gets hot** because it is so big that the pressure in its core is tremendous – enough to force the nuclei of hydrogen atoms to fuse (join together) to make helium atoms. This nuclear fusion reaction is like a gigantic nuclear bomb and it releases huge amounts of energy.

DID YOU KNOW?
The temperature of the Sun's surface is 6000°C. Each square centimetre burns with the brightness of 250,000 candles.

🌑 **Halfway between its core** and its surface, the Sun is as dense as water. Closer to the surface, it becomes as dense as air.

🌑 **Nuclear fusion reactions** in the Sun's core convert five million tonnes of gas into energy every second, but the energy takes ten million years to reach the surface.

193

Sunspots

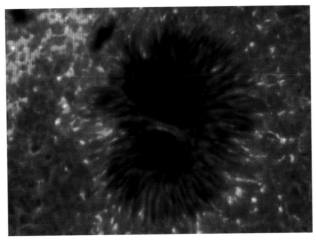

▲ Infrared photographs reveal the dark sunspots that appear on the surface of the Sun.

- **Dark spots on the Sun's photosphere** (surface) are called sunspots. They are 1500°C cooler than the rest of the surface.

- **The dark centre of a sunspot** is the umbra, the coolest part of a sunspot. Around it is the lighter penumbra.

- **Sunspots appear in groups** that seem to move across the Sun over two weeks, as the Sun rotates.

- **Small, individual sunspots** may last less than a day.

- **The number of sunspots** reaches a maximum every 11 years. This is called the solar or sunspot cycle.

🪐 **The next sunspot maximum** will be around 2011.

🪐 **When sunspots are at their maximum**, the Earth's weather may be warmer and stormier.

🪐 **Long-term sunspot cycles** last between 80 and 200 years.

🪐 **Observations of the Sun** by satellites, such as *Nimbus-7*, showed that less heat reaches the Earth from the Sun when sunspots are at a minimum.

DID YOU KNOW?

The SOHO satellite has probed beneath sunspots to reveal a whirlpool of sinking gas.

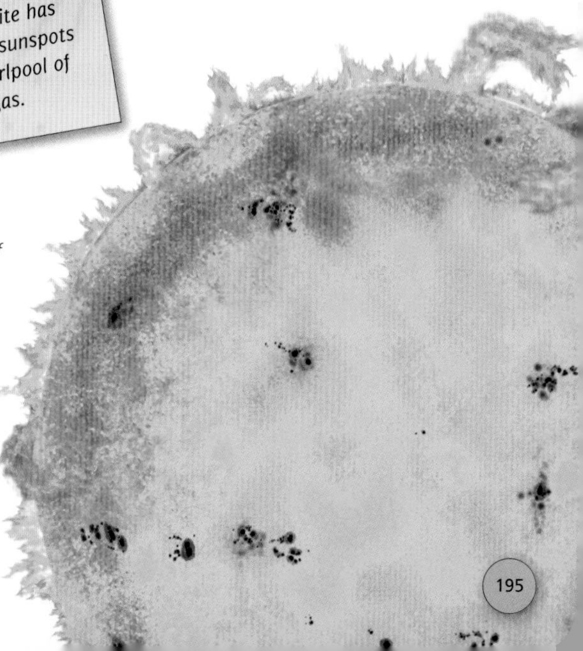

▶ *The Sun is a fiery ball of gas, mostly hydrogen and helium, made of several layers. Energy is produced in the central core and very slowly works its way outwards through a thick layer of gas. In the outer layer, the hot gas rises to the surface where heat and light escape into space.*

195

Solar eruptions

Solar flares are sudden eruptions on the Sun's surface. They flare up in just a few minutes, then take more than half an hour to die away again.

▼ Solar prominences can loop as far as 100,000 km out from the Sun's surface.

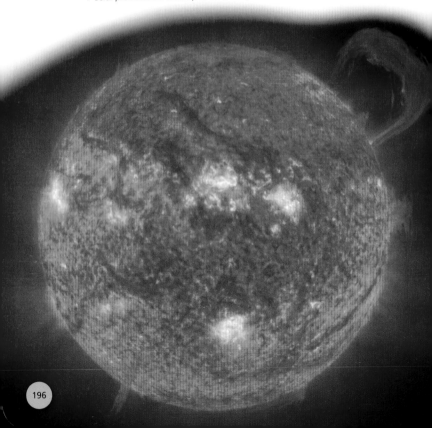

- **Solar flares reach temperatures** of 10 million°C and have the energy of billions of nuclear explosions.

- **They not only send out** heat and radiation, but also streams of charged particles.

- **The solar wind is the stream** of charged particles that shoots out from the Sun in all directions at speeds of over one million km/h. It reaches the Earth in several days, but also blows far throughout the Solar System.

- **Every second**, the solar wind carries away over one million tonnes of charged particles from the Sun.

- **Earth is shielded** from the lethal effects of the solar wind by its magnetic field.

- **Solar prominences** are gigantic arcs of hot hydrogen that sometimes spout out from the Sun.

- **Solar prominences reach temperatures** of 10,000°C.

- **Coronal mass ejections** are gigantic eruptions of charged particles from the Sun, creating gusts in the solar wind that set off magnetic storms on Earth.

- **Magnetic storms are massive hails** of charged particles that hit the Earth every few years or so, setting the atmosphere buzzing with electricity.

Solar changes

🪐 **The Sun is about 4.6 billion years old** and halfway through its life – as a medium-sized star it will probably live for around 11 billion years.

🪐 **Over the next few billion years**, the Sun will brighten and swell until it is twice as bright and 50 percent bigger.

🪐 **In five billion years**, the Sun's hydrogen fuel will have burnt out, and its core will start to shrink.

🪐 **As its core shrinks**, the rest of the Sun will swell up and its surface will become cooler and redder. It will be a red giant star.

🪐 **The Earth will have burnt** out long before the Sun is big enough to completely swallow it.

🪐 **The Sun will end** as a white dwarf.

🪐 **Between 1645 and 1715**, very few sunspots were seen on the Sun – called the Maunder minimum. At that time there was the Little Ice Age on Earth due to less heat from the Sun.

🪐 **More of the chemical carbon-14** is made on Earth when the Sun is less active. The carbon-14 is absorbed by trees, which means scientists can work out changes in solar activity in the past by measuring carbon-14 in old wood.

🪐 **The SOHO space observatory** is stationed between the Earth and the Sun, monitoring the Sun and changes in solar activity.

▶ *The Sun seems to burn steadily. In the short term, its brightness does seem to vary very slightly all the time, and over the next five billion years it will probably burn more ferociously.*

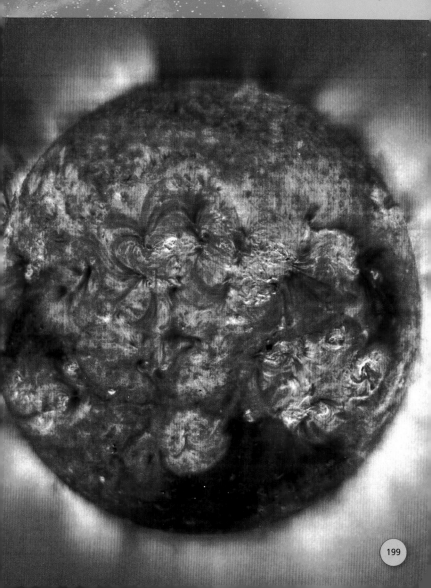

Planets

- **Planets are large globe-shaped objects** that orbit a star, such as the Sun.

- **They begin life** at the same time as their star, from the leftover clouds of gas and dust.

- **Planets are never** more than about five percent of the mass of the Sun. If they were bigger, they would be stars.

- **Some planets, called terrestrial planets**, have a surface of solid rock. Others, called gas planets, do not have a solid surface, just clouds.

- **The Solar System** has eight planets. Pluto was the ninth, but it is very small and is now called a planetoid (dwarf planet).

- **Over 200 planets** have been detected orbiting stars other than the Sun. These are called extra-solar planets.

- **Extra-solar planets** are too far away to see, but can be detected because they make their star appear to wobble.

- **Many known extra-solar planets** are giants, bigger than Jupiter. They orbit rapidly, closer to their stars than Mercury is to the Sun.

- **Improved detection techniques** may reveal smaller planets orbiting further out in space.

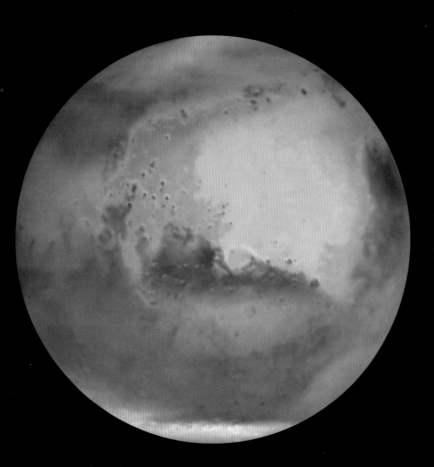

▲ *Probes, such as the Hubble telescope, are able to give scientists a more detailed view of the planets. Here, the Hubble has detected a storm on Mars.*

Moons

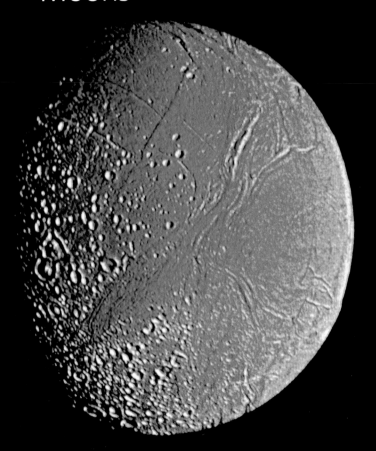

▲ *Saturn's moon, Enceladus, is marked by deep valleys, suggesting geological activity. This is quite rare in moons and smaller planets.*

- **Moons are the natural satellites** of planets. Most are small rock globes that continually orbit the planet, held in place by the planet's gravity.

- **There are more than 160 known moons** in the Solar System.

- **Every planet in the Solar System** has a moon, apart from Mercury and Venus, the nearest planets to the Sun.

- **New moons are frequently discovered**, as space probes such as the Voyagers reach distant planets.

- **Several moons have atmospheres**, including Saturn's moon Titan, Jupiter's Io, and Neptune's Triton.

- **Jupiter's moon Ganymede** is the largest moon in the Solar System.

- **The second largest** is Saturn's moon Titan. It is icy-cold, and is the only moon with a thick atmosphere of nitrogen gas.

- **The smallest moons** are icy lumps just a few kilometres across, rather like asteroids.

- **Saturn's moon, Iapetus**, is white on one side and black on the other.

- **Saturn's moon, Enceladus**, is only 500 km across, and its icy surface reflects almost all the sunlight.

Rotation

🪐 **Rotation means spinning**. Stars spin, planets spin, moons spin and galaxies spin – even atoms spin.

🪐 **The Earth takes 23.93 hours** to spin once. This is called its rotation period.

🪐 **The fastest-rotating planet** is Jupiter, which turns around once every 9.84 hours.

🪐 **The slowest-rotating planet** is Venus, which takes 243.01 days to turn around.

🪐 **The Sun takes 25.4 days** to rotate, but since the Earth is going around it too, it seems to take 27.27 days.

🪐 **As well as spinning**, space objects also move around each other. Moons orbit planets, planets orbit stars, and stars orbit the centre of galaxies.

🪐 **The Earth's movements** are not actually felt because everything is moving with it. However, the Earth's spin can be seen as the Sun, Moon and stars move across the sky.

🪐 **Gravity keeps everything** in orbit. The Sun's gravity pulls the Earth, and the Earth's gravity pulls the Moon.

DID YOU KNOW?
The fastest-spinning objects in the Universe are neutron stars – these can rotate 500 times in just one second!

▶ *Rotating galaxies are just part of the spinning, moving Universe.*

Years

🪐 **A calendar year is roughly the time** the Earth takes to travel once around the Sun – 365 days.

🪐 **The Earth actually takes 365.24219 days** to orbit the Sun. This is called a solar year.

🪐 **To compensate for the missing 0.242 days,** the Western calendar adds an extra day in February every fourth (leap) year.

🪐 **When measured by the stars**, not the Sun, Earth takes 365.25636 days to go round the Sun. This is because the Sun also moves a little, relative to the stars. This is called the sidereal year.

🪐 **Earth's perihelion** is the day its orbit brings it closest to the Sun – 3 January.

🪐 **Earth's aphelion** is the day it is furthest from the Sun – 4 July.

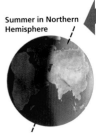

Summer in Northern Hemisphere

🪐 **The planet with the shortest year** is Mercury, which whizzes around the Sun in just 88 days.

🪐 **Neptune is the planet with the longest year**. It takes 164.8 years to orbit the Sun.

🪐 **The planet with the year** closest to Earth's in length is Venus – a year lasts 225 days.

🪐 **A year on Earth** is the time the Sun takes to return to the same height in the sky at noon.

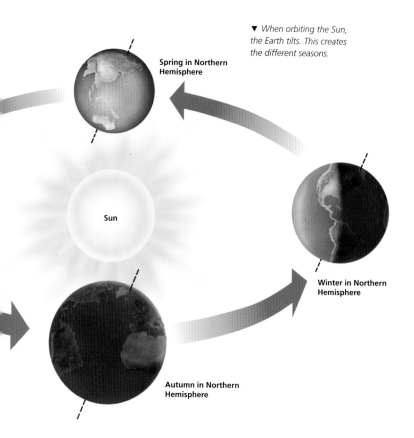

▼ *When orbiting the Sun, the Earth tilts. This creates the different seasons.*

Spring in Northern Hemisphere

Sun

Winter in Northern Hemisphere

Autumn in Northern Hemisphere

Day and night

▼ When it is daylight on the half of the Earth facing towards the Sun, it is night on the half of the Earth facing away from it. As the Earth rotates, the day and night halves shift gradually around the world.

- **The Earth turns eastwards** – this means that the Sun rises in the east as each part of the world spins round to face it.

- **As the Earth turns**, the stars come back to the same place in the night sky every 23 hours, 56 minutes and 4.09 seconds. This is a sidereal day (star day).

- **It takes 24 hours** for the Sun to come back to the same place in the daytime sky. This is the solar day, and it is slightly longer than the star day because the Earth moves one degree further round the Sun each day.

- **For each planet**, the length of day depends on how fast it spins and sometimes its speed in orbit.

- **Mercury spins once in 59 days**, but its solar day is 176 days because of its orbit.

- **A day on Jupiter** lasts less than ten hours because Jupiter spins so fast.

- **A day on Mars** is 24.6 hours – similar to a day on Earth.

DID YOU KNOW?
A day on the Moon lasts nearly one Earth month.

Solar calendar

🪐 **The Earth's orbit around the Sun** on a tilted axis causes the Sun to appear to gradually rise and fall in the sky during the year. This effect causes the 'midnight sun' phenomenon that is experienced at high latitudes near the poles.

🪐 **A solstice** (which comes from the Greek for 'sun stop') is the point at which the Sun appears to stop rising or falling and stands still in the sky.

🪐 **The summer solstice,** which occurs on 21 June, marks the Sun's most northerly extension above the Equator. At noon on 21 June the Sun is directly overhead at the Tropic of Cancer.

🪐 **The winter solstice**, which occurs on 21 December, marks the Sun's most southerly extension below the Equator. At noon on 21 December the Sun is directly overhead at the Tropic of Capricorn.

- **An equinox** (which means 'equal night') marks both the time and place at which the Sun crosses the Equator. During an equinox, everywhere on the planet has exactly 12 hours of daylight and 12 hours of darkness.

- **The vernal equinox** occurs around 21 March each year, and marks when the Sun crosses the Equator from south to north.

- **The vernal equinox** is used as the zero point in the celestial co-ordinate system.

- **On 23 September** each year, the autumn equinox occurs, which marks the Sun crossing the Equator from north to south.

▼ *Our understanding of the close link between astronomy and the calendar goes back a long way – some of the standing stones at Stonehenge in England (built about 2000 BC) are aligned with the position of the rising Sun at the summer solstice.*

Atmosphere

- **The gases held around a planet** by its gravity make up the atmosphere.

- **Every planet in the Solar System** has an atmosphere.

- **Each atmosphere** is very different. Earth's atmosphere is the only one that humans can breathe.

- **Atmospheres are not fixed**, but can change rapidly.

- **Moons are generally too small** and their gravity is too weak to have an atmosphere. However, some moons have one, including Saturn's moon Titan.

- **The primordial (earliest) atmospheres** came from the cloud of gas and dust surrounding the young Sun.

- **If Earth and the other rocky planets** had primordial atmospheres, they were stripped away by the solar wind (see solar eruptions).

▲ Jupiter's upper atmosphere contains bright curtains of light known as auroras (see auroras).

🪐 **Earth's atmosphere** was first formed from gases pouring out of volcanoes.

🪐 **Jupiter's atmosphere** is partly primordial, but it has been altered by the Sun's radiation, and the planet's own internal heat and lightning storms.

DID YOU KNOW?
The oxygen in Earth's atmosphere was formed entirely by plants.

▼ *Earth's unique atmosphere shields humans from the Sun's dangerous rays, as well as providing oxygen and water.*

213

Water

🌑 **Water is commonly found** as a solid, a liquid and a gas.

🌑 **A compound** of the elements hydrogen and oxygen, water has the chemical formula H_2O.

🌑 **Ice floats because water** is the only substance less dense (heavy) as a solid than as a liquid.

🌑 **Over 70 percent of the Earth's surface** is covered in water – this is why it looks blue from space.

🌑 **Water is fundamental** (basic) to all life – 70 percent of the human body is made up of water.

🌑 **Earth is the only planet** in the Solar System to have liquid water on its surface.

🌑 **Neptune has a deep ocean** of ionized water beneath its atmosphere of helium and hydrogen.

DID YOU KNOW?

The Earth's oceans cover more than 360 million km² of the planet.

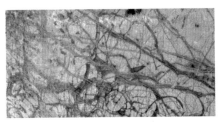

◀ Jupiter's moon, Europa, may have oceans of water beneath its icy surface, and it is a major target in the search for life in the Solar System.

🪐 **Dried-up riverbeds** show that Mars probably once had water on its surface. There is ice at both the poles and probably underground as well.

🪐 **In 1998**, a space probe found signs of frozen water on the Moon.

▼ *A satellite view of Iceland, which shows the land covered in snow and ice.*

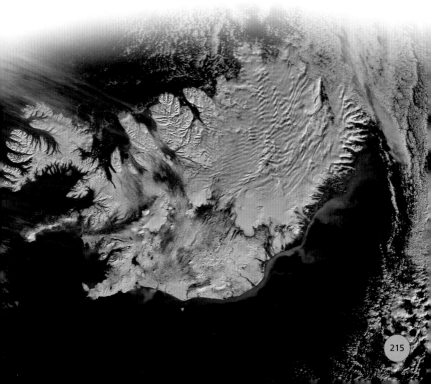

Tides

🪐 **Ocean tides are the rise and fall** of the water level in the Earth's oceans. They occur twice a day.

🪐 **The gravitational pull** of the Moon and the Sun create the tides on Earth.

🪐 **The Moon's pull** creates two bulges in the oceans – one below the Moon and one on the opposite side of the Earth.

🪐 **As the Earth spins**, the tidal bulges seem to move around the world, creating two high tides every day.

▼ *At high tide, the sea rises up the shore and dumps seaweed, shells and driftwood. Most coasts have two high tides and two low tides every day.*

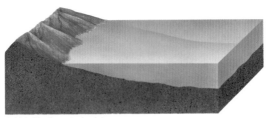

At high tide, the water level rises

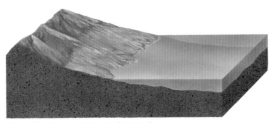

At low tide, the water level goes down again

🪐 **Spring tides are very high tides** that happen when the Sun and Moon are in line, and combine their pull.

🪐 **Neap tides are small tides** that happen when the Sun and Moon are at right angles to the Earth and their pulls are weakened by working against one another.

🪐 **The solid Earth has tides, too**, but they are very slight and the Earth only moves about 0.5 m.

🪐 **Tides are also any upheaval** created by the pull of gravity, as one space object orbits another.

🪐 **Moons orbiting large planets** undergo huge tidal pulls. Jupiter's moon, Io, is stretched so much that its interior is heated enough to create volcanoes.

🪐 **Whole galaxies can be affected** by tidal pulls, making them stretch as they are tugged by the gravitational pull of other passing galaxies.

▶ As the Moon spins around the Earth, Earth's oceans and seas are lifted by the Moon's gravity, creating a tidal bulge on opposing sides of the Earth.

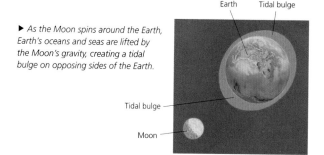

Earth   Tidal bulge

Tidal bulge

Moon

Mercury

- **The nearest planet to the Sun** is Mercury. During its orbit, it is between 45.9 and 69.7 million km away.

- **Mercury has the fastest orbit** – one orbit around the Sun takes just 88 Earth days.

- **Twice during its orbit**, Mercury gets very close to the Sun and speeds up so much that the Sun seems to go backwards in the sky.

- **Mercury rotates once every 58.6 days**, but the time between one sunrise and the next is 176 days, longer than its year.

- **Temperatures change** from −180°C at night to more than 430°C during the day (hot enough to melt lead).

- **The crust and mantle** are made largely of rock, but the core (75 percent of its diameter) is solid iron.

- **Mercury's dusty surface** is pocketed by craters made by space debris crashing into it.

- **With six percent of Earth's mass**, Mercury is so small that its gravity can only hold on to a very thin atmosphere.

▼ *The Sun looks huge as it rises over Mercury. The sunny side of the planet is boiling hot, but the night side is more than twice as cold as Antarctica.*

- **Mercury is so small** that its core has cooled and become solid (unlike Earth's). As this happened, Mercury shrank and its surface wrinkled.

- **Craters on Mercury** discovered by the USA's *Mariner 10* space probe have names such as Bach, Beethoven, Wagner, Shakespeare and Tolstoy.

▼ *Mercury is a planet of yellow dust, as deeply dented with craters as the Moon. Astronomers think that they have found ice in deep craters where the Sun never shines.*

The largest feature on Mercury is a huge impact crater called the Caloris Basin, which is about 1300 km across and 2 km deep

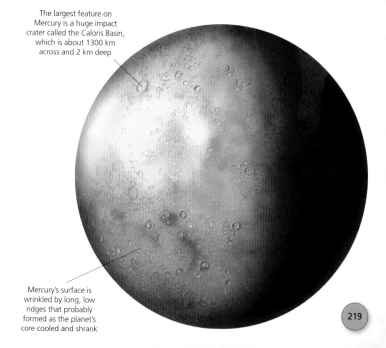

Mercury's surface is wrinkled by long, low ridges that probably formed as the planet's core cooled and shrank

219

Venus

🪐 **The second planet from the Sun** is Venus. Its orbit makes it 107.4 million km away at its nearest and 109 million km away at its furthest.

🪐 **Venus shines like a star** in the night sky because its thick atmosphere reflects sunlight amazingly well. This planet is the brightest object in the sky, after the Sun and the Moon.

🪐 **Venus is called the Evening Star** because it can be seen from Earth in the evening, just after sunset. However, it can also be seen before sunrise. It is visible at these times because it is quite close to the Sun.

🪐 **The atmosphere of Venus** is mostly carbon dioxide gas with thick clouds containing sulphuric acid, given out by the planet's volcanoes.

◀ The thick clouds of Venus are made of carbon dioxide gas and sulphuric acid. They reflect sunlight and make the planet shine like a star. None of its atmosphere is transparent like the Earth's, which makes it very difficult to see what is happening on the planet's surface.

▲ *The 6 km-high volcano on the surface of Venus is called Maat Mons. Images have been created on computer using radar data collected by the Magellan orbiter, which reached Venus in the 1990s.*

Venus is the hottest planet in the Solar System, with a surface temperature of more than 470°C.

Venus is so hot because the carbon dioxide in its atmosphere traps the Sun's heat. This overheating is called a runaway greenhouse effect.

The thick clouds hide its surface so well that until the Russian *Venera 9* probe landed on the planet in 1975, it was not known what was beneath the clouds.

Pressure on the surface of Venus is 90 times greater than that on Earth.

A day on Venus (the time it takes to spin around once) lasts 243 Earth days – longer than its year, which lasts 224.7 days. As Venus rotates backwards, the Sun comes up twice during the planet's yearly orbit – once every 116.8 days.

Venus is the nearest planet to Earth in size, measuring 12,102 km in diameter.

Earth

🌏 **The third planet out from the Sun**, the Earth, is 149.6 million km away on average.

🌏 **The Earth is the fifth largest planet** in the Solar System, with a diameter of 12,756 km and a circumference of 40,075 km at the Equator.

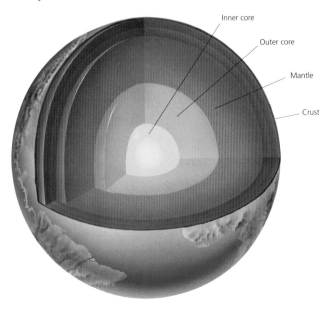

Inner core

Outer core

Mantle

Crust

▲ *The inner core at the centre of the Earth is made of iron. It is very hot and keeps the outer core as liquid. Outside this is the mantle, made of thick rock. The thin surface layer is called the crust.*

- **Along with Mercury, Venus and Mars,** the Earth is one of four rocky planets. It is made mostly of rock, with a core of iron and nickel.

- **No other planet in the Solar System** has liquid water on its surface, so Earth is uniquely suitable for life. More than 70 percent of Earth's surface is underwater.

- **The atmosphere is mainly harmless nitrogen** and life-giving oxygen, and it is over about 200 km deep. The oxygen has been made and maintained by plants over billions of years.

- **A magnetic field,** stretching 60,000 km out into space, protects Earth from the Sun's radiation.

- **The Earth formed 4.55 billion years ago** from clouds of space dust whirling around the young Sun. The planet was so hot that it was molten at first. The surface cooled slowly into a hard crust.

- **The Earth's orbit** around the Sun is 940 million km in length and takes 365.242 days.

- **Although the Earth is tilted** at an angle of 23.5 degrees, it orbits the Sun on a level plane – the plane of the ecliptic.

- **The Earth is made up** of the same basic materials as meteorites and the other rocky planets – mostly iron (35 percent), oxygen (28 percent), silicon (17 percent), magnesium (15 percent) and nickel (2.7 percent).

Earth's formation

- **The Solar System was created** when the gas cloud left over from a giant supernova explosion started to collapse in on itself and spin.

- **About 4.55 billion years ago**, only a vast, hot cloud of dust and gas circling a new star, the Sun, existed.

- **The Earth probably began** when tiny pieces of space debris (called planetesimals) were pulled together by each other's gravity.

- **As the Earth formed**, more space debris kept on smashing into it, adding new material. This debris included ice from the edges of the Solar System.

- **About 4.5 billion years ago**, a rock the size of Mars crashed into the Earth. The debris joined together to form the Moon.

- **The collision that created** the Moon made the Earth very hot.

- **Radioactive decay heated** the Earth even more.

- **For a long time**, the surface of the Earth was a mass of erupting volcanoes.

- **Iron and nickel melted** and sank to form the core.

- **Lighter materials**, such as aluminium, oxygen and silicon, floated up and cooled to form the crust.

DID YOU KNOW?
As the Earth rotates, it bulges in the middle like a pumpkin.

5 The Earth was made up of one large piece of land, but is now split into seven continents

▶ *The fiery young Earth gradually cooled until water condensed out of its steamy atmosphere to form oceans.*

1 Cloud starts to spin

4 Volcanoes erupt, releasing gases, which help to form the atmosphere

3 The Earth begins to cool and a hard shell forms

2 Dust gathers into balls of rock, which then form a small planet

Earth's atmosphere

- **Earth's atmosphere** is a blanket of gases, which we call air, that extends from the planet's surface up to a height of about 100 km.

- **Most of the air is concentrated** in the lowest part of the atmosphere. The air gets progressively thinner with increasing altitude. Above 7000 m, there is not enough oxygen for people to breathe.

- **Near the surface**, our atmosphere consists of nitrogen (78 percent), oxygen (21 percent) and small amounts of argon, carbon dioxide and other gases, together with a variable amount of water vapour.

- **The atmosphere is divided** into a series of layers that have different characteristics.

- **The lowest level is the troposphere**, which extends up to about 10 km above sea level. Weather and human activity are largely restricted to the troposphere.

- **The stratosphere extends** from 10 km to about 50 km in altitude, and contains the ozone layer that shields Earth's surface from the harmful ultraviolet (UV) radiation in sunlight.

- **Above the stratosphere** are the mesosphere (50–70 km) and the thermosphere (70–100 km). Most meteors that are seen burn up in the mesosphere or the upper stratosphere.

- **The uppermost level** of the atmosphere is called the exosphere and extends between 100–400 km above the Earth's surface. According to internationally accepted definitions, this part of Earth's atmosphere is actually in space.

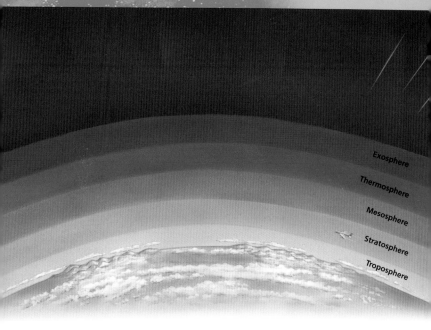

Exosphere

Thermosphere

Mesosphere

Stratosphere

Troposphere

▲ *The various layers of the atmosphere (not shown to scale) provide an insulating and protective bubble around the Earth.*

🪐 **The ionosphere** is the region around a planet that contains atoms and molecules that have been ionized by strong X-rays and UV light.

🪐 **Earth's ionosphere** extends from around 50 km above sea level out beyond the atmosphere to about 1000 km. The ionosphere contains a series of distinct layers (eg the Heaviside layer) that are used to reflect radio signals around the planet.

Magnetosphere

🪐 **Earth's magnetosphere** is the region of space within the influence of Earth's magnetic field. The magnetosphere shields the Earth from most of the effects of the solar wind.

🪐 **Despite its name, the magnetosphere** is not spherical but is shaped like an elongated teardrop with the rounded end of the teardrop facing towards the Sun.

🪐 **The sunward edge** of the magnetosphere is called the magnetopause and is located about 700,000 km from the Earth.

🪐 **Immediately to the sunward side** of the magnetopause is a shock wave (which is called the bow shock) that is caused by the solar wind being deflected by the magnetopause.

🪐 **On the side away from the Sun**, the magnetosphere trails away like the tail of a comet in what is known as the magnetotail.

🪐 **Although the magnetosphere deflects** most of the charged particles coming from the Sun and cosmic rays, some get through and become concentrated in two doughnut-shaped regions of radiation known as the Van Allen belts.

🪐 **Of the eight planets** in the Solar System, Venus and Mars are the only ones that do not have their own magnetosphere.

🪐 **Jupiter has by far the largest** magnetosphere and its magnetopause is located about 6 million km from the planet's surface.

🪐 **The magnetism of Earth's Moon** is too weak to produce a magnetosphere, but two of Jupiter's moons, Io and Ganymede, have magnetic fields of sufficient strength.

🪐 **Stars also produce magnetic fields** and have magnetospheres. The Sun's magnetosphere is called the heliosphere and its magnetopause (called the heliopause) has a radius of more than 80 AU.

▼ *Earth's magnetosphere (shown in blue, with the bow shock in purple) is shaped by the constant pressure of the solar wind.*

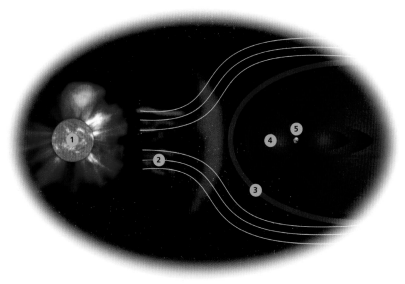

1 Sun	4 Magnetosphere
2 Solar Wind	5 Earth
3 Bow shock	

Auroras

- **Bright displays of shimmering light** called auroras appear at night over the North and South poles.

- **The aurora that appears** above the North Pole is Aurora Borealis, also known as the Northern Lights.

- **The aurora that appears** above the South Pole is Aurora Australis, or the Southern Lights.

- **Auroras are caused** by streams of charged particles from the Sun, known as the solar wind (see solar eruptions), crashing into the gases of the Earth's atmosphere.

- **Oxygen gas glows yellow-green** in colour when it is hit low in the atmosphere, and orange higher up.

- **Nitrogen gas glows bright red** in colour when hit normally, and bright blue when ionized.

- **A halo of light always exists** over each pole, but they are usually too faint to see. They flare up brightly when extra bursts of energy reach the Earth's atmosphere from the Sun.

- **Auroras only appear at the poles** because there are deep cracks in the Earth's magnetic field there.

- **When the solar wind** is blowing strongly, auroras are more spectacular.

- **New York and Edinburgh** get an average of ten aurora displays every year.

◄ The Northern Lights above the Arctic Circle look like curtains of bright colours.

The Moon

- **The Moon is 384,400 km** from the Earth and more than 25 percent of Earth's diameter.

- **Once every month**, the Moon orbits the Earth. Each orbit takes 27.3 days. It spins around once on its axis in exactly the same time, so only one side of the Moon's surface can be seen.

- **The Moon is the brightest object** in the night sky, but it does not give out any light itself. It shines only because its surface reflects sunlight.

- **One half of the Moon** is always lit by the Sun, but as it travels round the Earth, different amounts of the sunlit side can be seen. This is why the Moon seems to change shape. These are called the phases of the Moon.

- **A lunar month** is the time between one Full Moon and the next. This is slightly longer than the time the Moon takes to orbit the Earth because the Earth is also moving.

- **The Moon has no atmosphere** and its surface is simply dust, pitted with craters created by meteorites smashing into it early in its history.

New Moon   Crescent Moon   First quarter Moon   Gibbous Moon   Full Moon

▲ *During the first half of each monthly cycle, the Moon waxes (appears to grow) from a crescent-shaped New Moon to a Full Moon. During the second half, it wanes (dwindles) back to a crescent-shaped Old Moon.*

🪐 **On the Moon's surface** are large, dark patches called seas because that is what people once believed they were. They are actually lava flows from ancient volcanoes.

🪐 **One side of the Moon** is always turned away from the Earth and is called its far side. This is because the Moon spins round on its axis at exactly the same speed that it orbits the Earth.

▶ *Unlike the Earth's surface, which changes by the hour, the Moon's dusty, crater-pitted surface has remained much the same for billions of years. The only change happens when a meteorite smashes into it and creates a new crater.*

233

Lunar features

🌑 **Most of the craters on the Moon** were formed during a period of intense meteorite bombardment that began 4.5 billion years ago and ended 3.8 billion years ago.

🌑 **This intense meteorite bombardment** was followed by about 600 million years of volcanic activity when molten lava flooded out to cover the lunar seas. Since about 3.2 billion years ago, the Moon's surface has remained largely unchanged.

🌑 **Tycho (diameter 84 km)** is the most recent large crater and was formed only a few hundred million years ago.

▼ *Photographs from orbiting spacecraft reveal clear evidence of the numerous violent impacts that have shaped the Moon's surface features.*

▶ *The Moon is the only place that humans have ever visited in space. It has no atmosphere or wind, so the footprints created in its dusty surface in 1969 by the Apollo astronauts are still there today, perfectly preserved.*

One of the most prominent craters is Copernicus, which is a fine example of a ray-crater – it is surrounded by rays of pale material that were ejected from the crater by a meteorite impact.

Aside from areas of bare rock, most of the Moon's surface is covered by regolith – a mixture of dust and rock fragments that have been pulverized by meteorite impacts.

Much of the rock on the Moon is of a type called breccia and is composed of broken rock fragments that have been cemented together by lava.

Astronauts have collected nearly 400 kg of Moon rocks and brought them back to Earth for analysis and study.

The most unusual type of Moon rock is known as KREEP because it is rich in potassium (K), rare earth elements (REE) and phosphorous (P).

The Lunar Prospector spacecraft launched in 1998 detected traces of hydrogen near the Moon's poles and this may indicate the presence of small amounts of ice trapped in the rocks.

If there is any water at the lunar poles, then the most likely explanation is that it results from comets impacting on the Moon.

235

Eclipses

🪐 **When one space object,** such as the Moon, blocks out the light from another, such as the Sun, an eclipse occurs.

🪐 **A lunar eclipse** is when the Moon travels behind the Earth, and into the Earth's shadow (Earth is between the Moon and the Sun).

🪐 **Lunar eclipses happen** about once or twice a year and last only a few hours.

🪐 **In a total lunar eclipse,** the Moon turns rust-red.

🪐 **Lunar eclipses can be seen** from anywhere on the half of the Earth facing the Moon.

🪐 **A solar eclipse** is when the Moon comes between the Sun and the Earth, casting a shadow up to 270 km wide on to the Earth's surface.

Sun

▶ *Solar eclipse in Kenya, on 16 February 1980.*

🌑 **In a total eclipse of the Sun**, the Moon passes directly in front of the Sun, completely covering it so that only its corona can be seen (see the Sun).

🌑 **There are at least two solar eclipses every year**, but they are only visible from a narrow strip of the world.

🌑 **Totality is when the Moon** blocks out the face of the Sun completely. It only lasts for a few minutes.

🌑 **Solar eclipses are possible** because the Moon is 400 times smaller than the Sun, and is also 400 times closer to the Earth. This means the Sun and the Moon appear to be the same size in the sky.

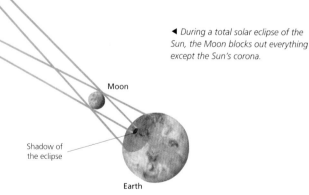

◄ During a total solar eclipse of the Sun, the Moon blocks out everything except the Sun's corona.

Moon

Shadow of
the eclipse

Earth

Mars

- **The nearest planet to Earth** after Venus is Mars. It has a daytime temperature and atmosphere more like the Earth's than any other planet.

- **Mars is called the red planet** because it is rust-red in colour. This comes from oxidized (rusted) iron in its soil.

- **The fourth planet out from the Sun**, Mars orbits at an average distance of 227.9 million km. It takes 687 Earth days to complete its orbit.

- **Mars is 6794 km in diameter** and spins around once every 24.62 hours – almost the same time as the Earth takes to rotate.

- **Olympus Mons, Mars' volcano**, is the biggest in the Solar System. It covers the same area as the UK and is three times higher than Mount Everest.

- **The surface of Mars** is dry, rocky and covered in dust. The wind blows up huge dust storms, sometimes covering the whole planet. Dust devils, similar to small tornadoes, often race across the surface of Mars.

- **Almost all the water on Mars** is frozen into ice. There are ice caps at the poles, and thin clouds made of ice crystals in the sky. Orbiting spacecraft have found ice hidden beneath the surface.

- **Mars was probably warmer** and wetter in the past. Spacecraft have spotted many dried-up riverbeds, gullies and lake beds, and the Mars Rovers, *Spirit* and *Opportunity*, have found minerals that normally form in water.

🪐 **The Mars Global Surveyor spacecraft** has discovered two gullies on Mars where water or mud may have gushed out onto the surface in the last few years.

🪐 **In 2008, NASA's Phoenix lander** confirmed the presence of water on the planet in the form of ice crystals just below the surface. The ice was found in a soil sample scooped from a 5-cm-deep trench nicknamed Snow White.

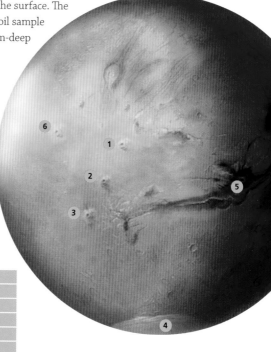

▶ *Mars is the best known planet besides Earth. Studies have revealed a planet with a surface like a red, rocky desert – but there is also plenty of evidence that Mars wasn't always so desert-like.*

| **1** Ascraeus Mons |
| **2** Pavonis Mons volcano |
| **3** Arsia Mons volcano |
| **4** Polar ice cap |
| **5** Vallis Marineris |
| **6** Olympus Mons volcano |

Martian moons

- **Mars has two small moons**: Phobos, which is about 27 km in diameter, and Deimos which is only about 15 km across. They have so little gravity that an astronaut could leap off them and into space using muscle power alone.

- **American astronomer Asaph Hall** (1829–1907) discovered the Martian moons in 1877. Hall was director of the US Naval Observatory and later became Professor of Astronomy at Harvard.

- **Phobos and Deimos** are highly irregular in shape. They have every appearance of being asteroids that were formed when the Solar System was created and were subsequently captured by Mars' gravity.

- **Both moons follow** very low regular orbits around the planet. Deimos is at an average distance of about 23,500 km, while Phobos orbits less than 6000 km above Mars' surface.

- **When viewed from the surface of Mars**, Phobos rises in the west and sets in the east twice each Martian day.

- **Large impact craters** caused by meteorites mark the surface of Phobos. The largest (named Stickney) is 10 km in diameter and extends across almost one-third of the moon's surface.

- **The meteorite craters** on Deimos have mostly been filled with dust and broken rock and none are more than 3 km across.

🪐 **Due to its extremely low orbit**, Phobos is being gradually slowed by Mars' gravity and is falling towards Mars' surface at a rate of 18 m per century. Phobos will crash into the surface of Mars in about 40 million years.

▼ *Phobos in close-up, showing the massive Stickney crater (at left) that dominates the moon's surface.*

Asteroids

- **Lumps of rock that orbit the Sun** are called asteroids. They are also known as minor planets.

- **Most asteroids are in the asteroid belt**, which lies between Mars and Jupiter. Some distant asteroids are made of ice and orbit the Sun beyond Neptune.

- **There are more than one million** asteroids bigger than one kilometer across. More than 200 asteroids are more than 100 km across.

- **A few asteroids** come near Earth. These are called Near Earth Objects (NEOs).

- **Asteroids were once known** as minor planets and new discoveries are recorded by the Minor Planet Center in Cambridge, Massachusetts, USA, which has given each one a unique catalogue number in addition to any name.

▼ Epsilon Eridani, a planetary system with two asteroid belts.

► Small asterioids are burnt up by the Earth's atmosphere every day. The chances of a big one colliding with us and destroying the Earth are remote.

🪐 **The first asteroid to be discovered** was Ceres in 1801. It was detected by Giuseppi Piazzi, one of the Celestial Police, whose mission was to find a 'missing' planet.

🪐 **At 940 km across** and 0.0002 percent of the Earth's mass, Ceres is the biggest asteroid.

DID YOU KNOW?

About every 50 million years, the Earth is hit by an asteroid measuring more than 10 km across.

🪐 **Two of the main belt asteroids**, (951) Gaspra and (243) Ida, were measured and photographed during a flyby of the *Galileo* spacecraft in 1993.

Asteroid belt

The asteroid belt is located at a distance of 2.1–3.3 AU from the Sun and contains many thousands of objects, of which some 30,000 have been individually identified.

Scientists believe that the main belt asteroids are planetismals left over from the formation of the Solar System. They were prevented from clumping together into a rock planet by the gravity of the massive gas planet Jupiter.

Only one of the main belt asteroids, (4) Vesta, is bright enough to be seen with the unaided eye.

▼ *Shown here between Jupiter (left) and Mars (right), the asteroid belt forms a near perfect circle around the Sun.*

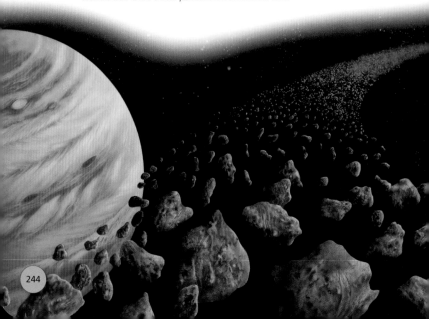

🪐 **Ida is one of the asteriods** photographed by the *Galileo* space probe. It has an irregular shape, 56 x 24 x 21 km, and is the only asteroid known to have its own natural satellite, Dactyl.

🪐 **A tiny asteroid**, Dactyl measures just one kilometre in diameter and orbits Ida at a distance of about 100 km.

🪐 **At the end of the 1990s**, the NEAR mission (Near Earth Asteroid Rendezvous) targeted two other asteroids, (253) Mathilde and (433) Eros. The spacecraft surveyed both asteroids from orbit before landing on the surface of Mathilde in 2001.

🪐 **The Trojan asteroids** are located at the outer edge of the main belt in two groups that are at 60 degrees to both the Sun and Jupiter.

🪐 **The first Trojan** to be discovered was named Achilles in 1906. Many Trojan asteroids are named after warriors from the ancient Greek tales of the Trojan wars.

🪐 **In addition to the Trojans**, some other asteroids also orbit in groups that are known as Hirayama families.

🪐 **These groups** are believed to be the remnants of larger asteroids that were smashed to pieces by collisions.

Jupiter

🪐 **The biggest planet in the Solar System**, Jupiter, is twice as heavy as all the other planets put together.

🪐 **Jupiter has no surface** for spacecraft to land on because it is made mostly of hydrogen and helium gas. The massive pull of Jupiter's gravity squeezes the hydrogen so hard that it is actually a liquid.

🪐 **Towards Jupiter's core**, immense pressure makes the liquid hydrogen behave like a metal.

🪐 **The ancient Greeks** originally named the planet Zeus after the king of their gods. Jupiter was the Roman name for Zeus.

🪐 **Jupiter spins around** in less than ten hours, which means that the surface is moving at nearly 50,000 km/h.

🪐 **The middle of Jupiter bulges out** because it spins so fast. It churns up the planet's metal core and generates a magnetic field, ten times stronger than the Earth's.

🪐 **Jupiter has a Great Red Spot** – a huge swirl of red clouds, measuring more than 40,000 km across. The scientist Robert Hooke first noticed the spot in 1644.

🪐 **Jupiter is so big that the pressure** at its core makes it very hot. The planet gives out heat, but not enough to make it glow. If it were 100 times bigger, nuclear reactions would occur at its core and turn it into a star.

🪐 **From 1995 to 2003**, the *Galileo* space probe orbited Jupiter and sent back data on the planet and its moons.

Great Red Spot

▲ *Jupiter is a gigantic planet, 142,984 km across. Its orbit takes 11.86 years and varies between 740.9 and 815.7 million km from the Sun. Its surface is often pierced by huge lightning flashes and thunderclaps, and temperatures here plunge to −150°C.*

Galilean moons

🌑 **The Galilean moons** are the four biggest of Jupiter's moons. They were discovered by Galileo, centuries before astronomers identified the other, smaller ones.

🌑 **Ganymede is the biggest** of the Galilean moons. At 5262 km across, it is larger than the planet Mercury.

🌑 **Ganymede looks solid**, but under its shell of ice is 900 km of slushy ice and water.

🌑 **At 4806 km across**, Callisto is the second biggest moon.

🌑 **Callisto is scarred** with craters from bombardments early in the Solar System's life.

🌑 **Io is the third biggest moon** at 3642 km across.

🌑 **The surface of Io is a mass of volcanoes** caused by it being stretched and squeezed by Jupiter's massive gravity.

🌑 **The smallest of the Galilean moons** is Europa at 3138 km across.

Ganymede   Callisto   Io   Europa

▲ Galileo spotted Jupiter's four biggest moons in the 17th century. Their names are Ganymede, Callisto, Io and Europa. Jupiter also has 59 other smaller moons and they are all very small and icy. Only 44 have been given names.

🪐 **Europa has a smooth icy surface** full of cracks, but the *Galileo* probe discovered an ocean of water under the ice where there might be living creatures.

▼ *Io's yellow glow comes from sulphur, which is thrown out as far as 300 km upwards by the moon's volcanoes.*

Saturn

- **The second biggest planet** in the Solar System is Saturn. It is 764 times as big in volume as Earth and measures 120,000 km in diameter.

- **Saturn takes 29.5 years** to travel around the Sun, so Saturn's year is 29.46 Earth years. The planet's complete orbit is a journey of more than 4.5 billion km.

- **Winds ten times stronger** than a hurricane on Earth swirl around Saturn's equator, reaching up to 1800 km/h.

- **Saturn is named after Saturnus**, the ancient Roman god of harvest. He was celebrated in the Roman festival of Saturnalia.

- **Saturn is not solid** but is made of gases and liquids, almost entirely hydrogen and helium. Only in the planet's very small core is there any solid rock.

- **As Saturn is so big**, the pressure deep inside is enough to turn hydrogen gas into a liquid. Further down, extreme pressure makes the liquid hydrogen act like a metal.

- **Saturn** is one of the fastest-spinning planets. Despite its size, it rotates in just 10.66 hours. This means that it spins at over 35,000 km/h.

🍃 **The surface of Saturn appears** smooth because the clouds are hidden under a layer of haze. However, the Cassini probe has spotted lightning storms and a huge swirling storm near the pole.

🍃 **The *Cassini* probe went into orbit** around Saturn in 2004 for a four-year study of its clouds, rings and moons. It carried the *Huygens* probe, which dropped through the atmosphere of the largest moon, Titan, onto a surface so cold that the pebbles were made of solid ice.

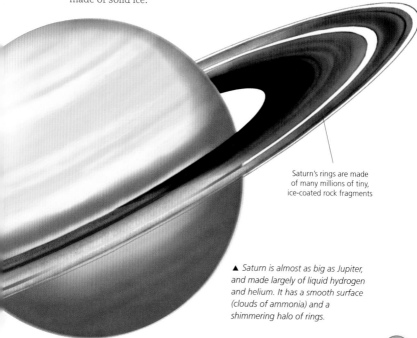

Saturn's rings are made of many millions of tiny, ice-coated rock fragments

▲ *Saturn is almost as big as Jupiter, and made largely of liquid hydrogen and helium. It has a smooth surface (clouds of ammonia) and a shimmering halo of rings.*

Saturn's rings

🪐 **The rings of Saturn** are made of chunks of ice, dust and tiny rocks that orbit the planet around its equator.

🪐 **When sunlight hits the ice**, the rings shimmer.

▼ *The icy chunks in Saturn's rings range in size from a marble to a car, each circling the planet in its own orbit.*

🪐 **The rings may be fragments** of a moon that was torn apart by Saturn's gravity before it formed properly.

🪐 **Galileo was the first** to see Saturn's rings, in 1610. However, Dutch scientist Christiaan Huygens (1629–1695) first realized that they were rings in 1659.

🪐 **There are two main sets** of rings – the A and the B rings.

🪐 **The A and B rings** are separated by a gap called the Cassini division because Italian astronomer Jean Cassini (1625–1712) spotted it in 1675.

🪐 **A third large ring** called the C or *crepe* ring was spotted closer to the planet in 1850.

🪐 **In the 1980s**, space probes revealed many other rings and 10,000 or more ringlets, some just 10 m in width.

🪐 **The rings are** (in order out from the planet) D, C, B, Cassini division, A, F, G and E. The A ring has its own gap called the Encke division.

DID YOU KNOW?

Saturn's rings measure more than 270,000 km across, but are very thin at just 100 m or less.

Shepherd moons

- **Shepherd moons** are small natural satellites that determine the shape and internal structure of the rings around giant gas planets.

- **The gap in Saturn's rings**, known as the Encke Division, is swept clear of ring material by the planet's smallest and innermost moon, Pan, which was not discovered until images from *Voyager 2* were re-examined in 1990.

- **The orbit of the shepherd moon Atlas**, which is only 32 km in diameter, maintains the sharp outer edge of Saturn's D ring.

- **Two shepherd moons**, Pandora and Prometheus, orbit on either side of Saturn's outermost F ring. These two moons sometimes swap orbits, and this gives the F ring a unique braided appearance.

- **The *Voyager 2* mission** discovered a similar arrangement around Uranus. Two shepherd moons, Cordelia and Ophelia, maintain the shape of the planet's outermost Epsilon ring.

- **Jupiter's four inner moons** (Metis, Adrastea, Almalthea and Thebe) are believed to be responsible for the origin and shape of the planet's ring system.

- **Scientists believe** that Jupiter's bright main ring is largely composed of material thrown up from the surfaces of Adrastea and Metis by meteorite impacts.

- **Jupiter's hazy outer ring** is often called the Almalthea Gossamer ring and is thought to be composed of fine dust from the surface of this moon.

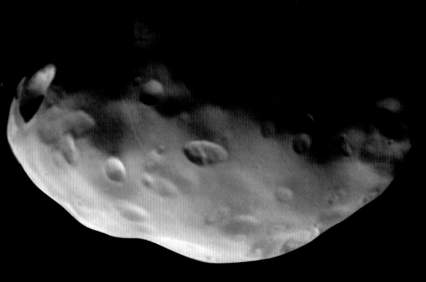

▲ *Although the irregularly shaped shepherd moon Pandora is only about 100 km long, it is massive in comparison to the ring particles, the largest of which measure about 10 m across.*

Around Neptune, Despina acts as the inner shepherd moon for the planet's Leverrier ring while Larissa is the inner shepherd for the more prominent Adams ring.

The outer edge of the Adams ring is marked by pronounced 'wiggles' that astronomers believe are caused by the gravitational influence of the moon Galatea.

Uranus

🪐 **Uranus is the seventh planet** out from the Sun. Its orbit keeps it 2870 million km away on average and takes 84 years to complete.

🪐 **It tilts so far on its side** that Uranus seems to roll around the Sun. The angle of its tilt is 98 degrees, so its equator runs vertically. This tilt may be the result of a collision with a meteor or another planet many years ago.

🪐 **In summer on Uranus**, the Sun does not set for 20 years. In winter, darkness lasts for over 20 years. In autumn, the Sun rises and sets every nine hours.

▶ The third largest planet in the Solar System, Uranus is 51,118 km across with a mass 14.54 times that of Earth. The planet spins around once every 17.24 hours, and it is the only planet to lie on its side. As it orbits the Sun, first one pole, then the equator, and then the other pole, face the Sun.

🪐 **Uranus has more than 20 moons**, all named after characters from Shakespeare's plays. There are five large moons – Ariel, Umbriel, Titania, Oberon and Miranda. Ten smaller moons were discovered by the *Voyager 2* probe in 1986 and several more have been found since.

🪐 **As Uranus is so far from the Sun**, it is very cold with surface temperatures dropping to –210°C. Sunlight takes just eight minutes to reach Earth, but 2.5 hours to reach Uranus.

🪐 **Uranus' icy atmosphere** is made of hydrogen and helium. Winds circulate the planet at more than 600 km/h – six times as fast as hurricanes on Earth.

🪐 **The surface of Uranus** is not solid. Green-blue methane clouds surround the planet in an atmosphere of hydrogen and helium gas. Inside Uranus is an icy mixture of water, ammonia and methane, and a small, rocky core.

🪐 **Uranus is only faintly visible** from Earth. It looks like a very faint star with the naked eye, and was not identified until 1781 (see Herschel).

🪐 **Uranus was named** after the ancient Greek god of the sky.

▶ *Uranus' moon, Miranda, looks as though it has been blasted apart, then put back together again.*

Neptune

🌰 **The eighth planet out from the Sun** is Neptune. Its distance varies from 4456 to 4537 million km.

🌰 **Neptune was discovered in 1846.** Two mathematicians, Englishman John Couch Adams and Frenchman Urbain Le Verrier, told astronomers where to look after they worked out where a new planet should be from the effect of its gravity on Uranus.

🌰 **Neptune is so far from the Sun** that its orbit lasts 164.79 Earth years. It has not yet completed one orbit since it was discovered in 1846.

🌰 **Like Uranus,** Neptune is shrouded in blue methane clouds at −210°C in a deep atmosphere made of hydrogen and helium gas.

🌰 **Unlike Uranus,** which is perfectly blue, Neptune has white clouds, created by heat inside the planet.

🌰 **Neptune has the strongest winds** in the Solar System, blowing at up to 2000 km/h.

◄ *Neptune's moon, Triton, is green, while its icecaps of frozen nitrogen are pink. It also has volcanoes that erupt fountains of ice. It is the coldest place in the Solar System with a surface temperature of −236°C.*

Great Dark Spot

▲ Neptune is the fourth largest planet. At 49,528 km across, it is slightly smaller than Uranus, but it is actually a little heavier. Like Uranus, its clouds of incredibly cold methane make it blue in colour. Neptune also has a thin layer of rings, but they are level and not at right angles to the Sun.

🪐 **The eight largest moons** are named after characters from Greek myths. Five additional small moons have been discovered recently but haven't yet been named.

🪐 **The Great Dark Spot** was a giant storm seen by *Voyager 2* in 1989, but it has since disappeared.

259

Pluto and Charon

- **When it was discovered in 1930**, Pluto became the ninth planet, but it was by far the smallest.

- **Since 2006**, Pluto has been classified as a dwarf planet by the International Astronomical Union (IAU). This means it fails to dominate its orbit around the Sun.

- **This new ruling** was further strengthened by the discovery of more objects of similar size to Pluto in the outer Solar System.

- **Pluto is further out** than the eight main planets, orbiting between 4437 and 7376 million km from the Sun.

- **At this distance**, Pluto takes 248 years to travel once around the Sun, even at an average speed of 17,100 km/h. It spins around in 6.4 Earth days, so its day lasts nearly as long as an Earth week.

- **Its orbit is squashed** into an oval shape, less circular than the eight main planets, and it is also tilted. This brings Pluto closer to the Sun than Neptune for about 20 years in each orbit.

◀ Pluto and Charon with the New Horizons spacecraft. The spacecraft will examine Pluto and Charon and provide scientists with new information.

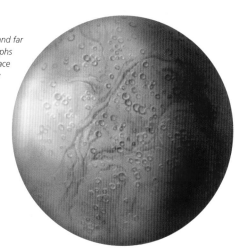

▶ *Pluto is so small and far away that photographs from the Hubble space telescope show very little detail. Dark and light patches can be seen, but astronomers don't know what these indicate. However, a twinkling of starlight around the edge of the planet shows that it must have some kind of atmosphere.*

🪐 **Unlike its gas giant neighbours,** Pluto is a tiny ball of rock covered by ice, with frozen methane on the surface.

🪐 **When nearest to the Sun,** Pluto has a very thin atmosphere, but when it is further away, the atmosphere freezes into ice on the surface.

🪐 **In 1978, American astronomer James Christy** discovered that Pluto had a large moon, which was named Charon. Then in 2005, two tiny moons, Nix and Hydra, were discovered.

🪐 **Four other dwarf planets** have been named, Ceres, Eris, Makemake and Haumea. Ceres is the largest of the asteroids between Mars and Jupiter.

🪐 **Eris is slightly larger** than Pluto, making it the largest dwarf planet.

Other planetoids

🪐 **Objects in the Kuiper Belt**, including Pluto and Charon, are often termed Trans-Neptunian Objects (TNOs) because they are located beyond the orbit of the planet Neptune.

🪐 **More than 700 Kuiper Belt Objects** (KBOs) have been discovered, but scientists believe that there are as many as 70,000 KBOs that are more than 100 km in diameter.

🪐 **In 1992**, the first KBO was discovered and given the designation QB1. The informal term cubewano is now used to refer to any of the KBOs in the densest part of the belt.

🪐 **The largest known cubewano** is Makemake (initially nicknamed 'Easter Bunny' because it was discovered at Easter), which was discovered in 2005. Makemake is about three-quarters the size of Pluto, although it appears only one-fifth as bright.

🪐 **At least three other KBOs** with diameters greater than 1000 km have been identified in the main part of the belt – Quaoar (1200 km), KX76 (1200 km) and Ixion (1065 km).

🪐 **In the outer reaches of the Kuiper Belt** (more than 80 AU from the Sun), astronomers have recently discovered several objects that rival or exceed Pluto in size.

🪐 **The largest of these distant objects** is Eris (formerly designated 2003 UB), which has a diameter of about 2500 km and a single moon, Disnomia.

🐚 **Another of these objects**, named Sedna to honour the Inuit goddess of the sea, is travelling away from the Sun and in 2114 will become the most distant named object in the Solar System.

🐚 **Objects known as Centaurs** are large asteroids, up to 500 km in diameter, which orbit the Sun between Jupiter and Neptune. Some astronomers believe that the Centaurs are Kuiper Belt objects that have been displaced as the result of collisions.

▲ *Schwassmann-Wachmann 1 is a comet that is believed to be a Centaur.*

Comets

- **Bright objects with long tails**, comets can sometimes be seen glowing in the night sky.

- **They may look spectacular**, but a comet is just a ball of ice a few kilometres in diameter.

- **Many comets orbit the Sun**, but their orbits are very long and they spend most of the time in the far reaches of the Solar System. They can be seen when their orbit brings them close to the Sun for a few weeks.

- **A comet's tail is made** as it nears the Sun and begins to melt. A vast plume of gas millions of kilometres long is blown out by the solar wind. The tail is what you see, shining as sunlight catches it.

- **Comets called periodics** appear at regular intervals.

- **Some comets reach speeds** of 2 million km/h as they near the Sun.

- **Far away from the Sun**, comets slow down to about 1000 km/h – that is why they stay away for so long.

- **The visit of the Hale-Bopp comet** in 1997 gave one of the brightest views of a comet since 1811, visible even from brightly lit cities.

- **The Shoemaker-Levy 9 comet** smashed into Jupiter in July 1994, with the biggest crash ever witnessed.

- **The most famous comet** of all is Halley's comet.

▶ *The* Rosetta *spacecraft and its lander following a comet.*

▼ *As it nears the comet's surface, the* Rosetta *lander gathers information about the comet.*

265

Halley's comet

🌀 **Halley's comet** is named after the British scientist Edmund Halley (1656–1742).

🌀 **He predicted that the comet** would return in 1758, which was 16 years after his death. It was the first time a comet's arrival had been predicted.

🌀 **Halley's comet orbits** the Sun every 76 years.

🌀 **Its orbit loops** between Mercury and Venus, and stretches out beyond Neptune.

🌀 **The Chinese described** a visit of Halley's comet as long ago as 240 BC.

🌀 **When Halley's comet** was seen in AD 837, Chinese astronomers wrote that its head was as bright as Venus and its tail stretched right through the sky.

🌀 **King Harold of England** saw the comet in 1066. When he was defeated by William the Conqueror a few months later, people interpreted the comet's visit as an evil omen.

▼ *Halley's comet was embroidered on the Bayeux Tapestry, which shows Harold's defeat by William.*

DID YOU KNOW?

Halley's comet was seen in about 12 BC, so some say it was the Bible's Star of Bethlehem.

▲ Halley's comet came close to Earth in 1986. Its next visit will be in 2061.

267

Meteors

🪐 **Streaks of light** seen in the night sky are meteors. They are made when dust or rocks crash into the Earth's atmosphere and burn up leaving a fiery trail.

🪐 **Meteoroids are the billions of tiny rocks** that hurtle around the Solar System. Most are no bigger than a pea.

🪐 **Most meteoroids are very small** and burn up when they enter the Earth's atmosphere.

🪐 **Shooting stars may look** like stars shooting across the night sky, but they are actually meteors.

🪐 **Meteor showers are bursts** of dozens of shooting stars that occur as Earth hits dust left by a comet.

🪐 **Although meteors are not stars**, meteor showers are named after the constellations they seem to come from.

🪐 **The heaviest showers** are the Quadrantids (3–4 January), the Perseids (12 August) and the Geminids (13 December).

DID YOU KNOW?

The impact of a large meteorite may have chilled the Earth and wiped out the dinosaurs.

🪐 **Meteorites are larger space rocks** that penetrate right through the Earth's atmosphere and reach the ground.

🪐 **A large meteorite** could hit the Earth at any time.

▶ *Most meteorites that enter Earth's atmosphere burn up in the stratosphere to produce the bright streak of light we call a meteor.*

Meteorites

🐚 **Meteorites are small** (less than about 1000 tonnes) solid objects from space that have impacted with the surface of a planet or moon.

🐚 **The largest known meteorite** weighs more than 60 tonnes, and is still lying where it fell at Hoba West in Namibia, Africa.

🐚 **Discovered in Greenland** by the explorer Robert Peary in 1897, the largest meteorite on public display weighs 34 tonnes. Nicknamed 'The Tent', it is now in the Hayden Planetarium in New York.

🐚 **Meteorites found on Earth** can be divided into three main categories, popularly known as irons, stones and stony-irons.

🐚 **Irons, which used to be called siderites,** are composed almost entirely of the metals iron and nickel (or alloys of the two) and when found their outer surface is often covered with rust.

◄ *When cut, polished and treated with acid, a nickel-iron meteorite reveals distinctive patterning that is named Widmanstatten, after the Austrian mineralogist who discovered the phenomenon in 1804.*

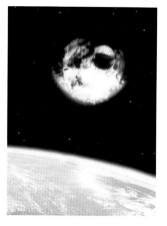

▶ *Most meteors burn away in the atmosphere, but some come crashing down to Earth.*

🪐 **Stones, which used to be called aerolites**, are composed of silicate minerals such as pyroxene, olivine and feldspar, together with a small amount of nickel or iron.

🪐 **There are two sub-types** of stony meteorites – chondrites, which often have a rounded appearance and a structure made up of tiny rock spheres known as chondrules, and achondrites, which usually have a jagged appearance and do not contain chrondrules.

🪐 **Stony-irons**, which used to be called siderolites, are composed of silicate minerals and nickel-iron in roughly equal proportions. Stony-irons are very rare and only about four percent of meteorites fall in this category.

🪐 **Tektites are small, rounded objects** made of silica glass. Previously thought to be meteorites, it is now accepted that tektites are produced by the impact of an asteroid striking Earth.

🪐 **The best places to find meteorites** are Antarctica and Western Australia because there has been so little human activity there.

271

Meteor craters

🪐 **The most famous** and best-preserved meteorite crater on Earth is the incorrectly named Meteor Crater in Arizona, USA, which measures 1265 m in diameter and is 175 m deep.

🪐 **A nickle-iron meteorite** about 50 m in diameter and weighing about 300,000 tonnes formed Meteor Crater. Most of the meteorite is still buried beneath the crater walls, although some fragments are on display in a local museum.

▼ *This crater in Arizona is one of the few large meteorite craters visible on Earth. The Moon is covered with them.*

- **Near Henbury in northern Australia** is a group of 13 separate craters that must have been formed by the fragments of a meteorite that broke up moments before it impacted the Earth.

- **Most meteorite craters** on the Earth's surface have been eroded almost out of existence, but geologists can still detect the telltale scars that are called as astroblemes ('star wounds').

- **Small meteorite impacts** cause distinctive horsetail-shaped features in rock that are known as shatter cones.

- **Measuring some 24 km across, the Ries crater** in southern Germany was caused by a meteorite about one kilometre in diameter. The town of Nördlingen is built on the dried-up bed of a lake that once filled the crater.

- **The 100-kilometre Manicouagan crater** in Canada is more than 200 million years old. A ring-shaped lake has formed around the 'peak' at the centre of this much-eroded crater.

- **Scientists have discovered** the remains of a 200-km crater beneath the sea floor off the coast of the Yucatàn Peninsula in the Gulf of Mexico. It is likely that this crater was caused by the asteroid strike that may have wiped out the dinosaurs 65 million years ago.

- **Seabed drilling has revealed** the existence of a crater 85 km in diameter beneath the waters of Chesapeake Bay on the east coast of the USA. The crater was identified by fragments of shocked quartz, which are only formed by meteorite impacts.

Constellations

Northern Hemisphere

▼ This projection shows the main constellations of the Northern Hemisphere, with the North Pole in the centre and the equator around the circumference.

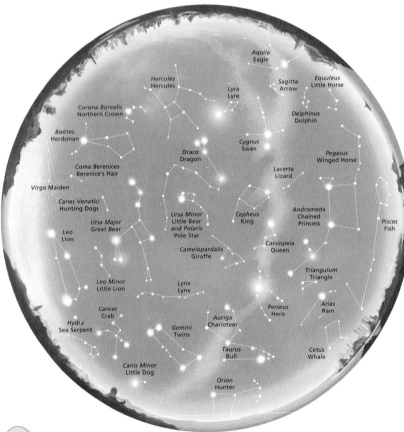

Aquila
Eagle

Hercules
Hercules

Lyra
Lyre

Sagitta
Arrow

Equuleus
Little Horse

Corona Borealis
Northern Crown

Delphinus
Dolphin

Boötes
Herdsman

Cygnus
Swan

Pegasus
Winged Horse

Coma Berenices
Berenice's Hair

Draco
Dragon

Lacerta
Lizard

Virgo Maiden

Canes Venatici
Hunting Dogs

Ursa Minor
Little Bear
and Polaris
Pole Star

Cepheus
King

Andromeda
Chained
Princess

Pisces
Fish

Leo
Lion

Ursa Major
Great Bear

Cassiopeia
Queen

Camelopardalis
Giraffe

Triangulum
Triangle

Leo Minor
Little Lion

Lynx
Lynx

Aries
Ram

Cancer
Crab

Auriga
Charioteer

Perseus
Hero

Hydra
Sea Serpent

Gemini
Twins

Cetus
Whale

Canis Minor
Little Dog

Taurus
Bull

Orion
Hunter

★ **In the Northern Hemisphere,** the constellations appear to revolve slowly across the sky in a counter-clockwise direction, making one complete revolution each year. This apparent motion is the result of the Earth's orbit around the Sun.

★ **The number and position of the constellations** that can be seen on any particular night depends on a number of factors – the time of year, the geographical latitude of the observer, and the direction of view.

★ **Constellations such as Ursa Minor and Draco** are described as circumpolar and are visible throughout the year.

★ **Other constellations,** such as Leo and Boötes, appear to rise and fall in the sky and may be below the observer's horizon for part of the year.

★ **The constellation of Orion,** which is situated on the celestial equator, is clearly visible from both the Northern and Southern hemispheres.

Star charts

The Northern and Southern hemisphere star charts give only approximate positions of the constellations and their stars.

These pages list all of the 88 constellations that can be found in the sky. The patterns are not fixed and the shape of all the constellations will change over time.

While some constellations are visible from only the Northern Hemisphere or the Southern Hemisphere, others can be seen from both.

Southern Hemisphere

▼ *This projection shows the main constellations of the Southern Hemisphere, with the South Pole in the centre and the equator around the circumference.*

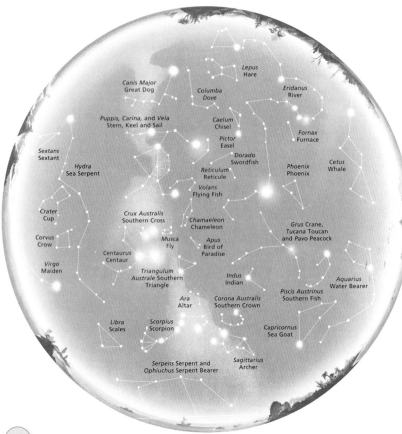

★ **In the Southern Hemisphere**, the constellations appear to revolve slowly across the sky in a clockwise direction, making one complete revolution each year. On average, stars rise about two hours earlier each month.

★ **The Southern Hemisphere sky** contains more bright stars than can be seen from the Northern Hemisphere. For example, the star Achenar in Eridanus is much too far south to be visible from either Europe or the USA.

★ **The Milky Way** appears much brighter in the Southern Hemisphere because of the tilt of the Earth's own axis of rotation.

★ **The Large Magellanic Cloud** in the constellation of Dorado is in fact another galaxy located about 157,000 light years away.

★ **Constellations** such as Hydrus are described as circumpolar and are visible throughout the year.

★ **Sirius in Canis Major** is the brightest star in the sky. It is best seen in the early morning during October, and in the late evening during January.

★ **The constellation of Virgo** is divided by the celestial equator and is consequently visible from both the Northern and Southern hemispheres.

★ **Crux Australis, the Southern Cross**, is one of the brightest constellations in the sky with three stars brighter than 2nd magnitude, but it is invisible from Europe or North America.

Andromeda

Chained Princess

The constellation Andromeda is one of the 48 listed in Ptolemy's *Almagest*. In Greek mythology Andromeda was chained to a cliff by her mother, Cassiopeia, and was rescued by the hero Perseus.

Perseus the slayer

Andromeda's rescuer achieved his mythological fame by beheading the hideous gorgon Medusa, whose face could turn people to stone. Perseus has been a favourite subject for artists throughout the ages. This statue by the Italian sculptor Donatello stands in the city of Florence.

★ **Where** Northern Hemisphere.

★ **Location** Between the constellations of Cassiopeia and Pegasus.

★ **Best time to view** During the first week of November.

★ **Brightest star** Alpheratz (Alpha Andromedae) has a magnitude of 2.06 and is 72 light years away.

★ **Brightest star position** R.A. 00 08 23, Dec. +29 05 26.*

*For an explanation of R.A. and Dec. see Celestial sphere p184

Antlia

Air Pump

A small Southern Hemisphere constellation, Antlia is one of the 14 constellations added during the 1750s by Nicolas-Louis de La Caille. He observed the night skies from an observatory at the southern tip of Africa.

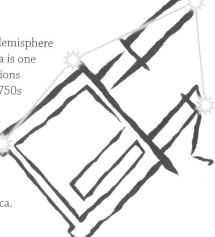

★ **Where** Southern Hemisphere.

★ **Location** Between the constellations of Hydra and Vela.

★ **Best time to view** During the last week of March.

★ **Brightest star** Alpha Antliae has a magnitude of 4.25.

★ **Brightest star position** R.A. 10 27 09, Dec. –31 04 14.

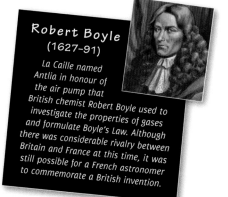

Robert Boyle (1627–91)

La Caille named Antlia in honour of the air pump that British chemist Robert Boyle used to investigate the properties of gases and formulate Boyle's Law. Although there was considerable rivalry between Britain and France at this time, it was still possible for a French astronomer to commemorate a British invention.

281

Apus
Bird of Paradise

A faint constellation, Apus is near the South Pole. It was among the first batch of new constellations that were added after the first European voyages across the Indian and Pacific oceans.

King bird of paradise

Dutch navigators in the 1590s named Apus for the spectacular birds of paradise, mainly found in New Guinea.

★ **Where** Southern Hemisphere.

★ **Location** Between the constellations of Triangulum Australe and Octans.

★ **Best time to view** During the last week of June.

★ **Brightest star** Alpha Apodis has a magnitude of 3.83.

★ **Brightest star position** R.A. 14 47 51, Dec. –79 02 41.

Aquarius
Water Bearer

Part of the zodiac, Aquarius is one of the oldest constellations in the sky. The ancient Greeks often associated Aquarius with Ganymede, who was the cupbearer of the gods.

★ **Where** Southern Hemisphere.

★ **Location** Between the constellations of Pisces and Capricorn.

★ **Best time to view** During the last week of September.

★ **Brightest star** Sadalsuud (Beta Aquarii) has a magnitude of 2.91.

★ **Brightest star position** R.A. 21 31 33, Dec. –05 34 16.

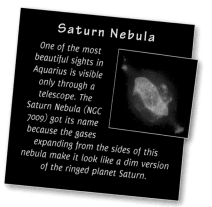

Saturn Nebula

One of the most beautiful sights in Aquarius is visible only through a telescope. The Saturn Nebula (NGC 7009) got its name because the gases expanding from the sides of this nebula make it look like a dim version of the ringed planet Saturn.

Aquila

Eagle

Ancient astronomers in
Babylonia identified
a number of
constellations,
including Aquila.
For the ancient Greeks, the eagle was
the symbol of Zeus, king of the gods.

Symbol of power

Eagles have long been
associated with
power. The chief god
of the Romans was
Jupiter, and each
of the Roman
legions carried
a golden eagle
as a symbol
of the military
power of Rome.

★ **Where** Northern and
Southern hemispheres.

★ **Location** Between the
constellations of Delphinus
and Scutum.

★ **Best time to view** During
the second week of August.

★ **Brightest star** Altair (Alpha
Aquilae) has a magnitude
of 0.77 and is 16 light years
away.

★ **Brightest star position**
R.A. 19 50 47, Dec. +08 52 06.

Ara

Altar

One of the
constellations
discovered by
Ptolemy was Ara. For the
Greeks, it was the altar of
Chiron who was the wisest
of the centaurs – mythical
creatures that were half-
human and half-horse.

★ **Where** Southern Hemisphere.

★ **Location** Between the
constellations of Telescopium
and Norma.

★ **Best time to view** During the
second week of July.

★ **Brightest star** Beta Arae has
a magnitude of 2.85.

★ **Brightest star position**
R.A. 17 25 18, Dec. –55 31 47.

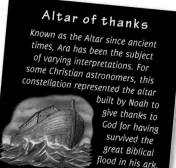

Altar of thanks

Known as the Altar since ancient
times, Ara has been the subject
of varying interpretations. For
some Christian astronomers, this
constellation represented the altar
built by Noah to
give thanks to
God for having
survived the
great Biblical
flood in his ark.

Aries

Ram

Identified by the Babylonians, Aries is one of the ancient zodiacal constellations. For the ancient Greeks it represented the ram that produced the fabulous Golden Fleece.

Golden Fleece

The mythical Golden Fleece may have some basis in fact. Archaeologists believe that ancient peoples put weighted-down sheepskins in rivers that flowed across gold-bearing rocks. Tiny particles of gold carried by the river became trapped in the wool and could then be combed out.

- ★ **Where** Northern and Southern hemispheres.
- ★ **Location** Between the constellations of Perseus and Pisces.
- ★ **Best time to view** During the middle of November.
- ★ **Brightest star** Hamal (Alpha Arietis) has a magnitude of 2.00.
- ★ **Brightest star position** R.A. 02 07 10, Dec. +23 27 45.

Auriga
Charioteer

Named by ancient Greek astronomers, Auriga represents Erechthonius, the legendary king of Athens. Erechthonius was credited with the invention of the four-horse chariot.

- ★ **Where** Northern Hemisphere.
- ★ **Location** Between the constellations of Taurus and Camelopardalis.
- ★ **Best time to view** During the last week of December.
- ★ **Brightest star** Capella (Alpha Aurigae) has a magnitude of 0.08 and is 42 light years away.
- ★ **Brightest star position** R.A. 05 16 41, Dec. +45 59 53.

For sport and war

Chariot racing was the most prestigious sport in the ancient World, but the chariot was much more than a piece of high-speed sporting equipment. Chariots were once used to carry heavily armed warriors into battle so that long distance marching did not make them too tired to fight.

287

Boötes

Herdsman

A very ancient
constellation,
Boötes was named
by the Babylonians.
For the Greeks,
the herdsman was
identified with
Boötes, son of the
goddess Demeter.

Turning the soil

The Greeks credited Boötes with the invention of the plough, which enabled them to grow wheat and barley in large fields. The basic design of the plough has not changed since ancient times, except that it is now drawn by tractors instead of by animals.

★ **Where** Northern Hemisphere.

★ **Location** Between the constellations of Coma Berenices and Corona Borealis.

★ **Best time to view** During the first week in June.

★ **Brightest star** Arcturus (Alpha Boötis) has a magnitude of −0.04 and is the brightest star in the Northern Hemisphere sky.

★ **Brightest star position** R.A. 14 15 40, Dec. +19 10 57.

Caelum

Chisel

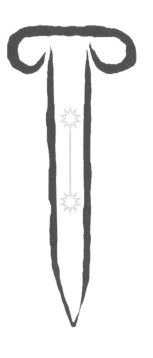

Originally named Caela Sculptoris, (the Sculptor's Chisel), Caelum is a Southern Hemisphere constellation. It was added by the French astronomer La Caille in the middle of the 18th century.

- ★ **Where** Southern Hemisphere.
- ★ **Location** Between the constellations of Columba and Eridanus.
- ★ **Best time to view** During the first week in January.
- ★ **Brightest star** Alpha Caeli has a magnitude of 4.45.
- ★ **Brightest star position** R.A. 04 40 33, Dec. −42 17 40.

Transforming instrument

The lowly chisel might not seem a likely candidate for stellar commemoration, but for La Caille it was an almost magical tool. In the hands of a skilled sculptor, the chisel could transform a block of stone into a beautiful statue.

289

Camelopardalis
Giraffe

In 1624, Camelopardalis was one of three new Northern Hemisphere constellations to be introduced by the German astronomer Jakob Bartsch. At this time the giraffe was believed to be a type of camel.

Biblical transport

Both the giraffe and the camel were exotic African creatures, but the camel also had Biblical associations. According to Bartsch, this constellation represented the camel that carried Rebecca across the desert to Isaac.

★ **Where** Northern Hemisphere.

★ **Location** Between the constellations of Auriga and Ursa Minor.

★ **Best time to view** During the middle of January.

★ **Brightest star** Beta Camelopardalis has a magnitude of 4.03.

★ **Brightest star position** R.A. 05 03 25, Dec. +60 26 32.

Cancer
Crab

The faintest of the zodiac constellations is Cancer. For the ancient Greeks, it represented the crab that was sent to distract the hero Hercules from completing one of his 12 labours.

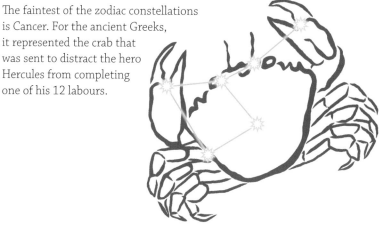

- ★ **Where** Northern and Southern hemispheres.
- ★ **Location** Between the constellations of Leo and Gemini.
- ★ **Best time to view** During the first week in March.
- ★ **Brightest star** Altarf (Beta Cancri) has a magnitude of 3.52.
- ★ **Brightest star position** R.A. 08 16 30, Dec. +09 11 08.

Beehive cluster

Located in the middle of the constellation, Cancer is an open cluster of about 200 stars that on dark nights can be seen by the unaided eye. Known to modern astronomers as M44, this cluster was named Praesepe (the Beehive) by the ancient Greeks.

Canes Venatici

Hunting Dogs

In 1687, Canes Venatici was introduced by the German astronomer Johannes Hevelius in his book *Uranographia*. It was one of seven new Northern Hemisphere constellations that he listed.

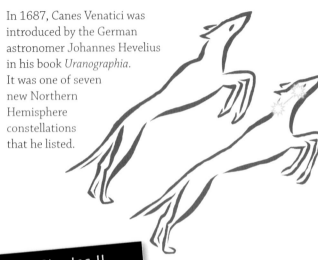

King Charles II

The brightest star in this constellation (which is actually a double star) was given the name Cor Caroli (the Heart of Charles) by the astronomer Edmond Halley in honour of his royal patron, Charles II of England.

★ **Where** Northern Hemisphere.

★ **Location** Between the constellations of Ursa Major and Coma Berenices.

★ **Best time to view** During the first week of May.

★ **Brightest star** Cor Caroli (Alpha Canum Venaticorum) has a magnitude of 2.90.

★ **Brightest star position** R.A. 12 56 02, Dec. +38 19 06.

Canis Major

Great Dog

According to Greek mythology, the Great Dog was the fastest running animal in the world and was placed in the sky to acknowledge this. Canis Major is one of the 48 constellations listed by Ptolemy.

★ **Where** Southern Hemisphere.

★ **Location** Between the constellations of Puppis and Lepus.

★ **Best time to view** During the first week of February.

★ **Brightest star** Sirius (Alpha Canis Majoris) has a magnitude of –1.46 and is the brightest star in the sky.

★ **Brightest star position** R.A. 06 45 09, Dec. –16 42 58.

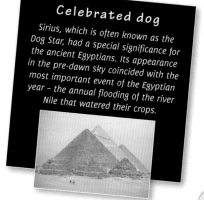

Celebrated dog

Sirius, which is often known as the Dog Star, had a special significance for the ancient Egyptians. Its appearance in the pre-dawn sky coincided with the most important event of the Egyptian year – the annual flooding of the river Nile that watered their crops.

Canis Minor

Little Dog

A small constellation, Canis Minor is associated with several Greek myths. In one version, the Little Dog sat patiently waiting to be fed beneath the table of the heavenly twins.

Hunter becomes hunted

According to another Greek myth, the Little Dog was one of the hounds that belonged to Actaeon the hunter, who offended the goddess Artemis. As punishment she turned Actaeon into a stag and he was pursued and devoured by his own hounds.

★ **Where** Northern and Southern hemispheres.

★ **Location** Between the constellations of Cancer and Monoceros.

★ **Best time to view** During the middle of February.

★ **Brightest star** Procyon (Alpha Canis Minoris) has a magnitude of 0.38 and is 11 light years away.

★ **Brightest star position** R.A. 07 39 18, Dec. +05 13 30.

Capricornus

Sea Goat

An ancient zodiacal constellation, Capricornus was first identified by Babylonian astronomers. They began the practise of depicting it as a goat with the tail of a fish.

- ★ **Where** Northern and Southern hemispheres.
- ★ **Location** Between the constellations of Aquarius and Sagittarius.
- ★ **Best time to view** During the first week of September.
- ★ **Brightest star** Deneb al-Giedi (Delta Capricorni) has a magnitude of 2.87 and is 49 light years away.
- ★ **Brightest star position** R.A. 21 47 02, Dec. −16 07 38.

Watery escape

In one Greek myth, a ferocious monster called Typhon was chasing the goatlike god Pan. The quick-thinking Pan jumped into the river Nile where the lower half of his body turned into a fish's tail so that he could swim away to safety.

Carina

Keel

Carina was once part of Ptolemy's constellation of Argo – the ship sailed by Jason and his crew. In the 18th century, astronomers dismantled Argo and divided the stars between several new constellations.

★ **Where** Southern Hemisphere.

★ **Location** Between the constellations of Crux Australis and Puppis.

★ **Best time to view** During the first week of March.

★ **Brightest star** Canopus (Alpha Carinae) has a magnitude of –0.72 and is the second brightest star in the sky.

★ **Brightest star position** R.A. 06 23 57, Dec. –52 41 44.

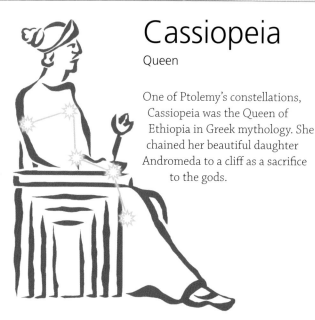

Cassiopeia
Queen

One of Ptolemy's constellations, Cassiopeia was the Queen of Ethiopia in Greek mythology. She chained her beautiful daughter Andromeda to a cliff as a sacrifice to the gods.

★ **Where** Northern Hemisphere.

★ **Location** Between the constellations of Andromeda and Cephus.

★ **Best time to view** During the first week of November.

★ **Brightest star** Gamma Cassiopeiae is a variable star and its current magnitude is 2.2.

★ **Brightest star position** R.A. 00 56 42, Dec. +60 43 00.

Face of Medusa

Cassiopeia was a proud and dishonest queen who suffered a terrible fate. When she went back on her promise to allow Perseus to marry her daughter Andromeda, he used the snake-haired head of the gorgon Medusa to turn Cassiopeia into stone.

Centaurus

Centaur

One of the largest constellations is Centaurus. Centaurs were beings that were half-human, half-horse. The ancient Greeks believed that Centaurus represented Chiron who, unlike other centaurs, was friendly towards humans.

★ **Where** Southern Hemisphere.

★ **Location** Between the constellations of Lupus and Hydra.

★ **Best time to view** During the middle of May.

★ **Brightest star** Alpha Centauri has a magnitude of –0.27 and is less than five light years away.

★ **Brightest star position** R.A. 14 39 37, Dec. –60 50 02.

Cepheus

King

According to Greek mythology, Cepheus was King of Ethiopia – Cassiopeia's husband and Andromeda's father. Cepheus is a small Ptolemaic constellation.

★ **Where** Northern Hemisphere.

★ **Location** Between the constellations of Cassiopeia and Draco.

★ **Best time to view** During the first week of October.

★ **Brightest star** Alderamin (Alpha Cephei) is 45 light years away and has a magnitude of 2.44.

★ **Brightest star position** R.A. 21 18 35, Dec. +62 35 08.

Starry gem

The star Mu Cepei has such a bright red colour that the astronomer William Herschel was reminded of a garnet and so called it the Garnet Star.

Cetus

Whale

Cetus is also known as the 'Sea Monster'. According to Greek mythology it was the sea monster that was sent to devour princess Andromeda.

Saved by the whale

Cetus may have been a sea monster to the Greeks, but for later astronomers this constellation represented the great 'fish' that swallowed the unfortunate Jonah when his shipmates threw him overboard.

★ **Where** Northern and Southern hemispheres.

★ **Location** Between the constellations of Eridanus and Pisces.

★ **Best time to view** During the middle of November.

★ **Brightest star** Diphda (Beta Ceti) has a magnitude of 2.04 and is 68 light years away.

★ **Brightest star position** R.A. 00 43 35, Dec. −17 59 12.

Chamaeleon

Chameleon

Introduced at the beginning of the 17th century, Chamaeleon was one of the new constellations to commemorate the exotic creatures that European explorers had encountered in Africa and Asia.

★ **Where** Southern Hemisphere.

★ **Location** Between the constellations of Apus and Volans.

★ **Best time to view** During the first week of April.

★ **Brightest star** Alpha Chamaeleontis has a magnitude of 4.07.

★ **Brightest star position** R.A. 08 18 31, Dec. –76 55 10.

Changing colours

Chameleons have the amazing ability to control their colouration by changing the size of special cells in their skin. When chameleons are feeling relaxed they are most likely to appear green, but they can turn yellow in a flash if they are angry.

Circinus

Drawing Compass

French astronomer Nicolas-Louis de La Caille named Circinus in the middle of the 18th century. Circinus comprises three faint stars that form a small triangle.

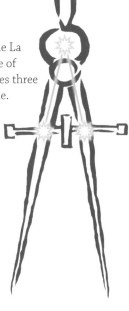

Measuring sea and sky

Drawing compasses, or dividers, had a double significance for La Caille. These instruments were used both by astronomers like himself, and also by the navigators who explored the oceans and were the first Europeans to see the wonders of the southern skies.

★ **Where** Southern Hemisphere.

★ **Location** Between the constellations of Triangulum Australe and Centaurus.

★ **Best time to view** During the first week of June.

★ **Brightest star** Alpha Circini has a magnitude of 3.19.

★ **Brightest star position** R.A. 14 42 28, Dec. −64 58 43.

Columba

Dove

Dutch philosopher and mapmaker Petrus Plancius identified and named Columba in 1605. It is a small constellation that lies just to the south of Canis Major.

★ **Where** Southern Hemisphere.

★ **Location** Between the constellations of Puppis and Caelum.

★ **Best time to view** During the last week in January.

★ **Brightest star** Phakt (Alpha Columbae) has a magnitude of 2.64.

★ **Brightest star position** R.A. 05 39 39, Dec. –34 04 27.

Bird of peace

Plancius named this constellation to commemorate the dove in the biblical account of the great flood. Noah sent a dove from the ark to see if the flood waters had receded. When the bird returned with an olive branch, Noah knew that there was dry land.

Coma Berenices

Berenice's Hair

Ptolemy named this constellation to honour Queen Berenice, who sacrificed a lock of her hair to ensure his safe return from overseas. Coma Berenices is the only constellation that refers to a real person.

Royal connection

Berenice was a member of the royal dynasty that ruled Egypt after the conquests of Alexander the Great. One of her descendants was Queen Cleopatra (left), who had famous love affairs with the Roman generals Julius Caesar and Mark Antony.

★ **Where** Northern and Southern hemispheres.

★ **Location** Between the constellations of Boötes and Virgo.

★ **Best time to view** During the first week of May.

★ **Brightest star** Beta Comae has a magnitude of 4.26 and is slightly brighter than Alpha Comae (4.32).

★ **Brightest star position** R.A. 13 11 52, Dec. +27 52 41.

Corona Australis

Southern Crown

Ancient Greek astronomers identified Corona Australis. For them, this constellation represented a victor's crown of woven laurel or olive leaves.

★ **Where** Southern Hemisphere.

★ **Location** Between the constellations of Sagittarius and Scorpius.

★ **Best time to view** During the first week of August.

★ **Brightest star** Meridiana (Alpha Coronae Australis) has a magnitude of 4.11.

★ **Brightest star position** R.A. 19 09 28, Dec. –37 54 16.

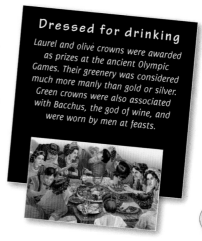

Dressed for drinking

Laurel and olive crowns were awarded as prizes at the ancient Olympic Games. Their greenery was considered much more manly than gold or silver. Green crowns were also associated with Bacchus, the god of wine, and were worn by men at feasts.

Corona Borealis

Northern Crown

There are two crowns in Ptolemy's list of constellations. Corona Borealis is the larger one. According to Greek legend, this northern crown was the golden crown of King Minos of Crete.

The Minotaur

In Greek legend, King Minos' wife Pasiphae gave birth to a monstrous child, the Minotaur, which had a human body and a bull's head. Minos imprisoned the Minotaur inside a labyrinth he constructed beneath his palace at Knossos in Crete.

★ **Where** Northern and Southern hemispheres.

★ **Location** Between the constellations of Hercules and Boötes.

★ **Best time to view** During the first week of July.

★ **Brightest star** Alphekka (Alpha Coronae Borealis) has a magnitude of 2.23.

★ **Brightest star position** R.A. 15 34 41, Dec. +26 42 53.

Corvus

Crow

One of the initial Greek constellations, Corvus is also called 'the Raven'. For the ancient Greeks, it was the bird sent by the god Apollo to spy on a woman named Coronis with whom he had fallen in love.

★ **Where** Northern and Southern hemispheres.

★ **Location** Between the constellations of Hydra and Crater.

★ **Best time to view** During the last week of April.

★ **Brightest star** Minkar (Gamma Corvi) has a magnitude of 2.59.

★ **Brightest star position** R.A. 12 15 48, Dec. −17 32 31.

Rat-tailed galaxies

Within the constellation of Corvus are two distant galaxies (NGC 4038 and NGC 4039) that are in the process of colliding. When viewed through a telescope, both galaxies appear to have long thin 'tails', and this has earned them the nickname of 'rat-tailed'.

Crater

Cup

Sitting in the sky alongside
Apollo's spy Corvus,
Crater represented
the god's personal
drinking cup.
It is another of
Ptolemy's original 48
constellations.

Sign of wealth

In ancient Greece, only the wealthiest
individuals could afford a metal
drinking cup and
these were prized
possessions. Most
people had to make
do with cheaper cups
made from baked
clay, although these
were often beautifully
decorated.

★ **Where** Northern and
   Southern hemispheres.

★ **Location** Between the
   constellations of Corvus
   and Sextans.

★ **Best time to view** During
   the last week of April.

★ **Brightest star** Alkes (Alpha
   Crateris) has a magnitude
   of 4.08.

★ **Brightest star position**
   R.A. 10 59 46, Dec. −18 17 56.

Crux Australis

Southern Cross

Despite being
the smallest
constellation, Crux
Australis makes a
strikingly bold pattern in
the sky. European astronomers did not
identify it as a constellation until 1679.

- ★ **Where** Southern Hemisphere.
- ★ **Location** Between the constellations of Centaurus and Carina.
- ★ **Best time to view** During the first week of May.
- ★ **Brightest star** Acrux (Alpha Crucis) has a magnitude of 0.83 and is 360 light years away.
- ★ **Brightest star position** R.A. 12 26 26, Dec. −63 05 56.

National symbol

Often shortened simply to Crux, the Southern Cross has become a symbol of the Southern Hemisphere. This easily recognizable constellation appears on the flags of several nations including Australia (pictured), New Zealand and Samoa.

Cygnus
Swan

For the ancient Greeks
Cygnus represented the
god Zeus in the form of a
swan. It got its name from
Ptolemy's list, but is often
called the 'Northern Cross'
because of its shape.

Continent in space

In Cygnus, the nebula NGC 7000 has
been nicknamed the 'North America
Nebula'. Although it appears as a
formless glowing
cloud to the unaided
eye, photographs
taken through
telescopes reveal
it to be shaped
like a map of
North America.

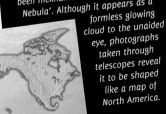

★ **Where** Northern Hemisphere.
★ **Location** Between the
constellations of Cepheus
and Draco.
★ **Best time to view** During the
last week of August.
★ **Brightest star** Deneb (Alpha
Cygni) has a magnitude of 1.25
and is 1800 light years away.
★ **Brightest star position**
R.A. 20 41 26, Dec. +45 16 49.

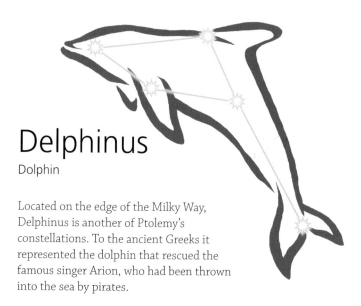

Delphinus
Dolphin

Located on the edge of the Milky Way, Delphinus is another of Ptolemy's constellations. To the ancient Greeks it represented the dolphin that rescued the famous singer Arion, who had been thrown into the sea by pirates.

★ **Where** Northern and Southern hemispheres.

★ **Location** Between the constellations of Equuleus and Sagitta.

★ **Best time to view** During the first week of September.

★ **Brightest star** Rotanev (Beta Delphini) has a magnitude of 3.54.

★ **Brightest star position** R.A. 20 37 32, Dec. +14 35 43.

Named in reverse

The two brightest stars in Delphinus were named Sualohcin and Rotanev by an Italian astronomer who called himself Nicholaus Venator. It took other astronomers a few years to realize that he named the stars using his own name spelt backwards.

KCAB OT TNORF

Dorado

Swordfish

In 1603, German astronomer Johann Bayer published *Uranometria*. Dorado is one of the Southern Hemisphere constellations that were first recorded in this star atlas.

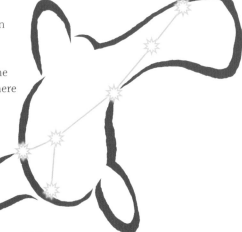

Sky spider

Dorado has two of the finest non-stellar objects in the sky. In addition to the Large Magellanic Cloud, it also contains the Tarantula Nebula (NGC 2070), which looks uncannily like a giant spider.

★ **Where** Southern Hemisphere.

★ **Location** Between the constellations of Volans and Reticulum.

★ **Best time to view** During the first week in January.

★ **Brightest star** Alpha Doradus has a magnitude of 3.27.

★ **Brightest star position** R.A. 04 34 00, Dec. –55 02 42.

Draco

Dragon

Among the constellations on Ptolemy's list, Draco was said to represent the dragon that was killed by the Greek hero Cadmus before he founded the city of Thebes. It is one of the largest constellations in the sky.

★ **Where** Northern Hemisphere.

★ **Location** Between the constellations of Lyra and Ursa Minor.

★ **Best time to view** During the first week of July.

★ **Brightest star** Gamma Draconis has a magnitude of 2.23 and is 100 light years away.

★ **Brightest star position** R.A. 17 56 36, Dec. +51 29 20.

Cat's eye

Draco is a popular subject for amateur astronomers because it contains the Cat's Eye Nebula (NGC 6543). With a good telescope, it is possible to see the oval shape and green colouration that gave this nebula its name.

Equuleus

Little Horse

In the Northern Hemisphere Equuleus is the smallest of the constellations. It was named by the Greek astronomer Hipparchus to represent the younger brother of the winged horse Pegasus.

Hermes' gift

According to Greek mythology Hermes, the wing-footed messenger of the gods, gave the Little Horse as a gift to Castor, who was one of the Heavenly Twins represented by the constellation of Gemini.

★ **Where** Northern and Southern hemispheres.

★ **Location** Between the constellations of Pegasus and Delphinus.

★ **Best time to view** During the first week of September.

★ **Brightest star** Kitalpha (Alpha Equulei) has a magnitude of 3.92.

★ **Brightest star position** R.A. 21 15 49, Dec. +05 14 52.

Eridanus

River

Eridanus has long been identified as a river in the sky. For the astronomers of ancient Babylonia, it represented the Euphrates River that provided vital irrigation water for crops.

★ **Where** Southern Hemisphere.

★ **Location** Between the constellations of Lepus and Cetus.

★ **Best time to view** During the middle of December.

★ **Brightest star** Achernar (Alpha Eridani) has a magnitude of 0.46 and is 85 light years away.

★ **Brightest star position** R.A. 01 37 43, Dec. −57 14 12.

Life-sustaining river

Unsurprisingly, ancient Egyptian astronomers believed that Eridanus represented the river Nile. It was the water and silt carried downstream by the annual flooding of the Nile that transformed barren riverbanks into fertile farmland.

Fornax

Furnace

A Southern Hemisphere constellation, Fornax was first recorded by French astronomer Nicolas-Louis de La Caille in the 1750s. It was originally named Fornax Chemica (the Chemical Furnace).

A loss to science

La Caille named Fornax to honour the famous French chemist Antoine Levoisier, who discovered and named the element oxygen. Unfortunately, this great scientist became very unpopular and he was guillotined during the French Revolution.

★ **Where** Southern Hemisphere.

★ **Location** Between the constellations of Caelum and Sculptor.

★ **Best time to view** During the first week of December.

★ **Brightest star** Alpha Fornacis) is a binary star with magnitudes of 4.0 and 7.0.

★ **Brightest star position** R.A. 03 12 04, Dec. −28 59 13.

Gemini

Twins

Listed by Ptolemy, Gemini is one of the ancient zodiacal constellations. According to Greek mythology, the twins were Castor and Pollux – the sons of Zeus and the Spartan princess Leda.

★ **Where** Northern and Southern hemispheres.

★ **Location** Between the constellations of Cancer and Auriga.

★ **Best time to view** During the first week of February.

★ **Brightest star** Pollux (Beta Geminorum) has a magnitude of 1.14 and is 36 light years away.

★ **Brightest star position** R.A. 07 45 19, Dec. +28 01 34.

Hooded face

The nebula NGC 2392 in Gemini was nicknamed the Eskimo Nebula by astronomers who thought that it looked like the face of an Inuit surrounded by a fur-lined parka hood.

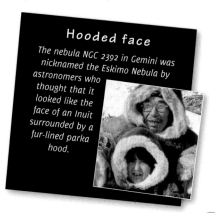

Grus

Crane

Symbolizing a long-necked bird, Grus is one of the Southern Hemisphere constellations that were introduced at the beginning of the 17th century. These constellations are sometimes called the Southern Birds.

Harbinger of spring

Grus was so named because the brightest stars resemble the shape of a long-necked bird in flight. In some myths and legends, the crane is a symbol of sunrise or the arrival of spring.

★ **Where** Southern Hemisphere.

★ **Location** Between the constellations of Phoenix and Microscopium.

★ **Best time to view** During the last week of September.

★ **Brightest star** Alnair (Alpha Gruis) has a magnitude of 1.74 and is 68 light years away.

★ **Brightest star position** R.A. 22 08 14, Dec. –46 57 40.

Hercules

Hercules

In Greek mythology, Hercules was the bravest and mightiest of all the heroes and he performed 12 famous tasks or labours. Hercules is one of the few constellations that carry the name of an individual.

- ★ **Where** Northern and Southern hemispheres.
- ★ **Location** Between the constellations of Lyra and Corona Borealis.
- ★ **Best time to view** During the middle of July.
- ★ **Brightest star** Kornephoros (Beta Herculis) has a magnitude of 2.77.
- ★ **Brightest star position** R.A. 16 30 13, Dec. +21 29 22.

Stellar traffic signals

The star Rasalgethi (Alpha Herculis) is a strangely colourful, multiple star. There is a giant red star with a bright green companion, and this star has its own tiny orange companion.

Horoligium

Clock

Representing
a pendulum
clock, Horologium is
a Southern Hemisphere
constellation. It was named
by Nicolas-Louis de La Caille
in the 1750s to credit some of
the technical advances that had
assisted the progress of science.

Measuring time

Accurate timekeeping is essential for astronomers, and Horologium was named to honour the world's first accurate mechanical clock – the pendulum clock invented in 1657 by the Dutch scientist Christiaan Huygens.

★ **Where** Southern Hemisphere.

★ **Location** Between the constellations of Reticulum and Phoenix.

★ **Best time to view** During the middle of December.

★ **Brightest star** Alpha Horologii has a magnitude of 3.18.

★ **Brightest star position** R.A. 04 14 00, Dec. –42 17 40.

Hydra

Sea Serpent

Listed by Ptolemy, Hydra is the biggest of all 88 constellations. In Greek mythology, the Hydra was not a sea serpent, but a nine-headed monster that was killed by Hercules.

★ **Where** Southern Hemisphere.

★ **Location** Between the constellations of Crater and Antilia.

★ **Best time to view** During the first week of April.

★ **Brightest star** Alphard (Alpha Hydrae), nicknamed the 'Solitary One', has a magnitude of 1.98.

★ **Brightest star position** R.A. 09 27 35, Dec. –08 39 31.

Many-headed monster

Slaying the swamp-dwelling Hydra was one of Hercules' famous 12 labours. Every time he cut off one of its heads, two more grew in its place. He finally defeated the Hydra by using a burning branch to stop it growing new heads.

Hydrus
Little Water Snake

Hydrus is a small constellation. The German astronomer Joachim Bayer added it to the list of constellations in 1603. It is situated between the Large and Small Magellanic clouds.

Sea snake

The Little Water Snake was named after the various snakes found in tropical oceans. The yellow-bellied sea snake (left) spends its whole life in water. Its venom is more powerful than that of any land snake.

★ **Where** Southern Hemisphere.

★ **Location** Between the constellations of Reticulum and Tucana.

★ **Best time to view** During the first week of December.

★ **Brightest star** Alpha Hydri has a magnitude of 2.80 and is 36 light years away.

★ **Brightest star position** R.A. 00 25 46, Dec. −77 15 15.

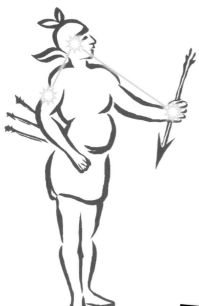

Indus
Indian

A constellation of the Southern Hemisphere, Indus is one of only two constellations that have an American connection. It was named by Dutch explorers to honour the Native Americans they encountered on their voyages.

★ **Where** Southern Hemisphere.

★ **Location** Between the constellations of Grus and Pavo.

★ **Best time to view** During the first week in September.

★ **Brightest star** Persian (Alpha Indi) has a magnitude of 3.11.

★ **Brightest star position** R.A. 20 37 34, Dec. –47 17 29.

Traditional lifestyle

Although most of the constellations named by Dutch navigators refer to Asia and Australasia, they also wanted to commemorate the various people of the American continents, such as those from whom they purchased the island of Manhattan.

Lacerta

Lizard

One of the few Northern Hemisphere constellations not among the 48 listed by Ptolemy is Lacerta. This celestial lizard was first identified and named in 1687 by the German astronomer Johannes Hevelius.

Celestial lighthouses

The constellation of Lacerta gave a part of its name to the incredibly bright BL-Lac objects. They send powerful beams of radiation sweeping across the Universe like a lighthouse's beams over the sea.

★ **Where** Northern Hemisphere.

★ **Location** Between the constellations of Cassiopeia and Cygnus.

★ **Best time to view** During the first week of October.

★ **Brightest star** Alpha Lacertae has a magnitude of 3.77.

★ **Brightest star position** R.A. 22 31 17, Dec. +50 16 17.

Leo

Lion

An ancient zodiacal constellation, Leo is the only one that looks remotely like its namesake. For the Greeks, it represented the Nemaean lion that was slain by the hero Hercules.

★ **Where** Northern and Southern hemispheres.

★ **Location** Between the constellations of Virgo and Cancer.

★ **Best time to view** During the first week of April.

★ **Brightest star** Regulus (Alpha Leonis) has a magnitude of 1.35 and is 85 light years away.

★ **Brightest star position** R.A. 10 08 22, Dec. +11 58 02.

Invulnerable opponent

The Nemaean lion was not only fierce and immensely strong, its skin was impervious to weapons. Hercules killed the beast with his bare hands, skinned it using one of its own claws, and later wore the skin as his own armour.

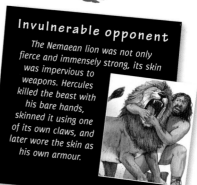

Leo Minor

Little Lion

Ancient astronomers did not consider Leo Minor to be a constellation. Johannes Hevelius first added it to the sky, along with Lacerta and five others, in the 17th century.

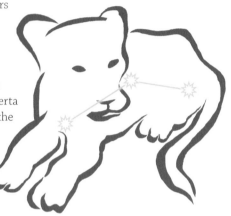

Rejected constellation

Hevelius stole some stars from Ursa Major to make his Little Lion, but some of his fellow astronomers wished that he hadn't. They thought the Little Lion should be rejected like some of the other constellations Hevelius invented, such as Cerberus (the three-headed dog).

★ **Where** Northern and Southern hemispheres.

★ **Location** Between the constellations of Ursa Major and Leo.

★ **Best time to view** During the first week of April.

★ **Brightest star** Praecipua (46 Leonis Minoris) has a magnitude of 3.83.

★ **Brightest star position** R.A. 10 53 19, Dec. +34 12 54.

Lepus

Hare

Lepus is one of the 48 constellations listed in Ptolemy's *Almagest*. It is situated beneath the constellation of Orion and was said to be the animal that he most liked to hunt.

★ **Where** Northern and Southern hemispheres.

★ **Location** Between the constellations of Canis Major and Eridanus.

★ **Best time to view** During the middle of January.

★ **Brightest star** Arneb (Alpha Leporis) has a magnitude of 2.58 and is 950 light years away.

★ **Brightest star position** R.A. 05 32 44, Dec. –17 49 20.

Lucky Lepus

The hare is widely recognized as representing vitality and good fortune. According to Chinese tradition, it was a hare in the Moon that made the elixir of immortality.

Libra
Scales

Libra is the only constellation of the zodiac named for an inanimate object. Some Greek legends associate it with Mochis, the inventor of weights and measures.

Balance of justice

For the ancient Egyptians, Libra represented the scales used to weigh the soul of a dead person. Subsequently, scales have come to represent the balance of justice, weighing the arguments for and against a defendant.

★ **Where** Northern and Southern hemispheres.

★ **Location** Between the constellations of Scorpius and Virgo.

★ **Best time to view** During the middle of June.

★ **Brightest star** Alpha Librae has a magnitude of 2.61 and is 72 light years away.

★ **Brightest star position** R.A. 15 17 00, Dec. −09 22 58.

Lupus

Wolf

A small constellation, Lupus was recorded in Ptolemy's list. Ancient Greek astronomers did not associate it with any particular wolf and it was thought to represent the idea of wildness.

- ★ **Where** Southern Hemisphere.
- ★ **Location** Between the constellations of Scorpius and Centaurus.
- ★ **Best time to view** During the middle of June.
- ★ **Brightest star** Men (Alpha Lupi) has a magnitude of 2.30.
- ★ **Brightest star position** R.A. 14 41 56, Dec. −47 23 17.

Spirit of savagery

The name Lupus is fairly modern. The ancient Greek and Roman astronomers called this constellation Therion, which was a non-specific fierce animal that might have been a wolf or a domestic dog that had become wild.

Lynx

Lynx

Introduced in 1689 by Hevelius, the Lynx is a Northern Hemisphere constellation. He named it, rather mischievously, because it was so faint that an astronomer needed the eyes of a lynx in order to see it.

Sharp-eyed animal

The lynx is a wildcat that has distinctive tufts on its ears. Because it usually hunts small prey high up in the mountains, the lynx has acquired a reputation for having exceptionally good eyesight.

★ **Where** Northern Hemisphere.

★ **Location** Between the constellations of Ursa Major and Gemini.

★ **Best time to view** During the last week in February.

★ **Brightest star** Alpha Lyncis has a magnitude of 3.13 and is 166 light years away.

★ **Brightest star position** R.A. 09 21 03, Dec. +34 23 33.

Lyra

Lyre

According to Greek mythology, Lyra represents the lyre presented by the god Apollo to the famous musician Orpheus. Lyra is situated on the edge of the Milky Way and is one of Ptolemy's 48 constellations.

★ **Where** Northern Hemisphere.

★ **Location** Between the constellations of Cygnus and Hercules.

★ **Best time to view** During the first week of August.

★ **Brightest star** Vega (Alpha Lyrae) has a magnitude of 0.03 and is the second brightest star in the northern sky.

★ **Brightest star position** R.A. 18 36 56, Dec. +38 47 01.

Ring Nebula

Between the stars Beta and Gamma, Lyrae is a fuzzy object that looks like an out of focus star and has been designated M31. Only by using high-powered telescopes can astronomers see the celestial beauty of the Ring Nebula.

Mensa

Table Mountain

The faintest of all the constellations, Mensa is one of the 14 Southern Hemisphere constellations introduced by La Caille. It is the only constellation that refers to a real geographical location – Table Mountain in South Africa.

Famous landmark

The French astronomer Nicolas-Louis de La Caille made his observations of the Southern Hemisphere skies during a visit to Cape Town in the 1750s. He thought it fitting to commemorate his visit by naming one of his new constellations after the city's most famous landmark.

★ **Where** Southern Hemisphere.

★ **Location** Between the constellations of Volans and Hydrus.

★ **Best time to view** During the middle of January.

★ **Brightest star** Alpha Mensae has a magnitude of 5.09.

★ **Brightest star position** R.A. 06 10 14, Dec. −74 45 11.

Microscopium
Microscope

All the stars that make up this constellation are very faint. Microscopium is another of La Caille's constellations that commemorates scientific instruments and technical advances – in this case the microscope, which was invented in about 1590.

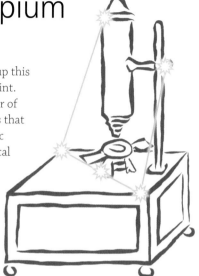

★ **Where** Southern Hemisphere.

★ **Location** Between the constellations of Piscis Austrinus and Sagittarius.

★ **Best time to view** During the first week of September.

★ **Brightest star** Gamma Microscopii has a magnitude of 4.67.

★ **Brightest star position** R.A. 21 01 17, Dec. –32 05 28.

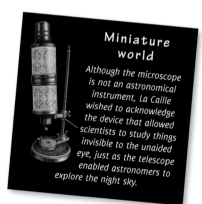

Miniature world

Although the microscope is not an astronomical instrument, La Caille wished to acknowledge the device that allowed scientists to study things invisible to the unaided eye, just as the telescope enabled astronomers to explore the night sky.

Monoceros

Unicorn

German astronomer Jakob Bartsch invented three constellations in 1624, one of which is Monoceros. Although the unicorn is a mythical creature, it does not appear in any of the Greek myths.

Christmas tree

At the very top of Monoceros is an open cluster of stars that has been catalogued as NGC 2264. A small telescope will reveal why this astronomical object is much better known by its nickname – the Christmas Tree Cluster.

- ★ **Where** Northern and Southern hemispheres.
- ★ **Location** Between the constellations of Canis Minor and Orion.
- ★ **Best time to view** During the first week of February.
- ★ **Brightest star** Beta Monocerotis has a magnitude of 3.7 and is a triple star.
- ★ **Brightest star position** R.A. 06 28 49, Dec. –07 01 58.

Musca

Fly

At the beginning of the 17th century Musca was among the constellations named by European navigators. They saw the Southern Hemisphere skies for the first time while sailing across the Indian and Pacific Oceans.

★ **Where** Southern Hemisphere.

★ **Location** Between the constellations of Chamaeleon and Crux Australis.

★ **Best time to view** During the first week of May.

★ **Brightest star** Alpha Muscae has a magnitude of 2.69.

★ **Brightest star position** R.A. 12 37 11, Dec. −69 08 07.

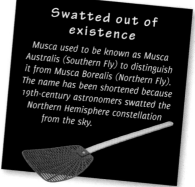

Swatted out of existence

Musca used to be known as Musca Australis (Southern Fly) to distinguish it from Musca Borealis (Northern Fly). The name has been shortened because 19th-century astronomers swatted the Northern Hemisphere constellation from the sky.

Norma

Square

La Caille first introduced Norma in his 1752 star atlas. He gave it this name because the three brightest stars form the shape of a right-angled set square – a tool used by builders and architects.

★ **Where** Southern Hemisphere.

★ **Location** Between the constellations of Ara and Circinus.

★ **Best time to view** During the middle of June.

★ **Brightest star** Gamma Normae has a magnitude of 4.02.

★ **Brightest star position** R.A. 16 19 50, Dec. –50 09 20.

Octans
Octant

A constellation of the
Southern Hemisphere,
Octans was created
by La Caille. He
named it to
commemorate
the invention
of the octant,
which was a forerunner of
the modern sextant.

★ **Where** Southern Hemisphere.
★ **Location** Between the
constellations of Hydrus
and Apus.
★ **Best time to view** During the
middle of September.
★ **Brightest star** Gamma
Octantis has a magnitude
of 3.76.
★ **Brightest star position**
R.A. 21 41 29, Dec. –77 23 24.

South Pole

The dim star
Sigma Octantis
is informally
known as the
south Pole
Star, although it is barely visible even
on the darkest nights. The first people
to stand directly below this star were
Roald Amundsen and his team of
Antarctic explorers in October 1911.

337

Ophiuchus

Serpent Bearer

Ophiuchus is one of Ptolemy's original 48 constellations. It got its name because it is closely entwined with the constellation of Serpens (the Serpent).

Fastest mover

Ophiuchus contains Barnard's Star, which is an extremely interesting red dwarf. It has the greatest proper motion of any known star, and moves against the background of the other stars by the apparent diameter of the Full Moon every 175 years.

★ **Where** Northern and Southern hemispheres.

★ **Location** Between the constellations of Hercules and Scorpius.

★ **Best time to view** During the middle of July.

★ **Brightest star** Rasalhague (Alpha Ophiuchi) has a magnitude of 2.08 and is 62 light years away.

★ **Brightest star position** R.A. 17 34 56, Dec. +12 33 36.

Orion
Hunter

Since the time of the ancient Babylonians, Orion has been identified as a constellation. For Greek astronomers it represented the great Orion, who was the mightiest of all the mythological hunters.

★ **Where** Northern and Southern hemispheres.

★ **Location** Between the constellations of Monoceros and Eridanus.

★ **Best time to view** During the middle of January.

★ **Brightest star** Rigel (Beta Orionis) has a magnitude of –0.12 and is 900 light years away.

★ **Brightest star position** R.A. 05 14 32, Dec. –08 12 00.

Celestial chess piece

There is a nebula in Orion designated IC 434 (or Barnard 33), but it is better known as the Horsehead Nebula. It was given this name because its shape looks like the knight in a standard chess set.

Pavo

Peacock

Introduced at the beginning of the 17th century, Pavo is one of the Southern Bird constellations. Although the peacock was already familiar to Europeans, it was considered sufficiently exotic to be part of the newly discovered Southern Hemisphere skies.

Hundred-eyed

According to Greek mythology Hermes, god of thieves, killed the goddess Hera's hundred-eyed watchman, Argus. Hera then placed Argus' eyes in the tail of the peacock as a reminder of her all-seeing servant.

★ **Where** Southern Hemisphere.

★ **Location** Between the constellations of Indus and Triangulum Australe.

★ **Best time to view** During the middle of August.

★ **Brightest star** Joo Tseo (Alpha Pavonis) has a magnitude of 1.94 and is 230 light years away.

★ **Brightest star position** R.A. 20 25 39, Dec. −56 44 06.

Pegasus

Winged Horse

Among the original
Greek constellations,
Pegasus is
connected to
the constellation
Andromeda.
To the ancient
Greeks it represented the
mythical flying steed Pegasus, which could
only be ridden by the hero Bellerophon.

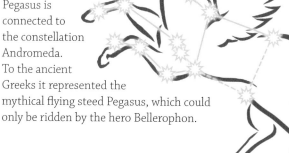

★ **Where** Northern and
Southern hemispheres.

★ **Location** Between the
constellations of Pisces
and Vulpecula.

★ **Best time to view** During
the first week of October.

★ **Brightest star** Enif (Epsilon
Pegasi) has a magnitude of
2.38 and is 520 light years
away.

★ **Brightest star position**
R.A. 21 44 11, Dec. +09 52 30.

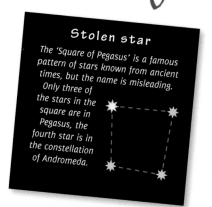

Stolen star

The 'Square of Pegasus' is a famous
pattern of stars known from ancient
times, but the name is misleading.
Only three of
the stars in the
square are in
Pegasus, the
fourth star is in
the constellation
of Andromeda.

Perseus

Hero

In Greek mythology it was Perseus who killed the Gorgon, Medusa. The constellation of Perseus represents the hero wielding his sword in one hand and holding Medusa's decapitated head in the other.

Stellar timekeeping

The star Algol (Beta Persei) is a variable star of the eclipsing binary type that has a very precise period. It changes its apparent magnitude (from 2.1 to 3.4) every 2 days 20 hours 48 minutes 56 seconds exactly.

★ **Where** Northern Hemisphere.

★ **Location** Between the constellations of Camelopardalis and Andromeda.

★ **Best time to view** During the middle of December.

★ **Brightest star** Mirphak (Alpha Persei) has a magnitude of 1.80 and is 620 light years away.

★ **Brightest star position** R.A. 03 24 19, Dec. +49 51 40.

Phoenix

Phoenix

One of the Southern Hemisphere constellations
identified during the European voyages
of discovery was the Phoenix.
Curiously, it is the only one
to have been
named after
a mythical
creature rather
than a real bird
or animal.

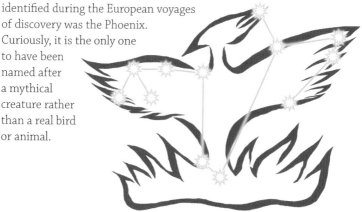

★ **Where** Southern Hemisphere.

★ **Location** Between the
constellations of Eridanus
and Grus.

★ **Best time to view** During the
first week of November.

★ **Brightest star** Ankaa (Alpha
Phoenicis) has a magnitude
of 2.39.

★ **Brightest star position**
R.A. 00 26 17, Dec. –42 18 22.

Immortal bird

In myths and legends,
the phoenix was
a bird with a
peculiar life-
cycle. Every 500
years or so the
phoenix would
set itself on fire
and be consumed
by the flames, only to be
immediately reborn from the ashes.

Pictor

Easel

Named by French astronomer Nicolas-Louis de La Caille, Pictor is a Southern Hemisphere constellation. In addition to commemorating scientific achievements, La Caille also wanted to honour the visual arts.

Confusing names

Originally named the Painter's Easel, this constellation is now known by the Latin name Pictor (Painter). However, in English it is usually referred to as the Easel.

★ **Where** Southern Hemisphere.

★ **Location** Between the constellations of Carina and Dorado.

★ **Best time to view** During the second week of January.

★ **Brightest star** Alpha Pictoris has a magnitude of 3.27 and is 78 light years away.

★ **Brightest star position** R.A. 06 48 11, Dec. −61 56 29.

Pisces

Fish

One of the ancient constellations of the zodiac, Pisces encompasses the vernal equinox (the place where the Sun crosses the celestial equator every year). Throughout the ages it has been variously represented as either one or two fish, and it has no well known mythological connections.

- ★ **Where** Northern and Southern hemispheres.
- ★ **Location** Between the constellations of Aries and Aquarius.
- ★ **Best time to view** During the first week of November.
- ★ **Brightest star** Alpherg (Eta Piscium) has a magnitude of 3.62.
- ★ **Brightest star position** R.A. 01 31 29, Dec. +15 20 45.

Bracelet of stars

The ring of bright stars situated at the western end of Pisces is a group of stars that has been recognized since ancient times. Once known as the Jewelled Bracelet, it is now called the Circlet.

Piscis Austrinus

The Southern Fish

Among the 48 constellations listed in Ptolemy's *Almagest* is Piscis Austrinus. Although this fish does not appear in Greek mythology, it was often depicted on early star maps drinking the water poured by Aquarius.

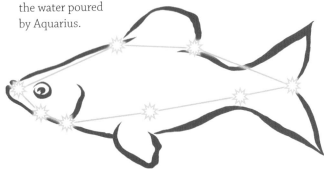

King of Persia

Astronomers in ancient Persia believed that Fomalhaut, which is sometimes called the Solitary One, was one of the 'royal' stars that protected their king and safeguarded the entrance to heaven.

★ **Where** Northern and Southern hemispheres.

★ **Location** Between the constellations of Sculptor and Capricornus.

★ **Best time to view** During the first week of October.

★ **Brightest star** Fomalhaut (Alpha Piscis Austrini) has a magnitude of 1.16 and is 22 light years away.

★ **Brightest star position** R.A. 22 57 39, Dec. −29 37 20.

Puppis
The Stern

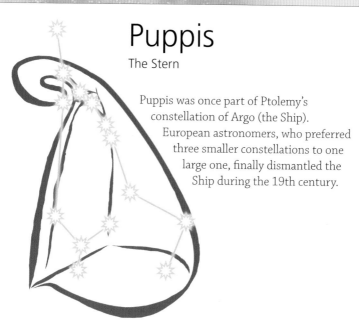

Puppis was once part of Ptolemy's constellation of Argo (the Ship). European astronomers, who preferred three smaller constellations to one large one, finally dismantled the Ship during the 19th century.

★ **Where** Southern Hemisphere.

★ **Location** Between the constellations of Vela and Columba.

★ **Best time to view** During the last week of February.

★ **Brightest star** Suhail Hadar (Zeta Puppis) has a magnitude of 2.25 and is 2400 light years away.

★ **Brightest star position** R.A. 08 03 35, Dec. –40 00 12.

Unused name

Puppis contains a distant cluster of stars that has been designated M93. One 19th century astronomer suggested that the bright stars in this cluster make the shape of a starfish, but the name Starfish Cluster was not adopted by his colleagues.

Pyxis
Mariner's Compass

As a result of his observations in South Africa, La Caille invented 14 new constellations, including Pyxis. Some of the stars in the compass were taken from Ptolemy's constellation of Argo.

Pointing the way

The Mariner's Compass seems an obvious choice for the name of a constellation to commemorate the European voyages of exploration that 'discovered' the South Seas. La Caille was probably unaware that the magnetic compass was in fact invented in China.

★ **Where** Southern Hemisphere.

★ **Location** Between the constellations of Antia and Puppis.

★ **Best time to view** During the middle of February.

★ **Brightest star** Alpha Pyxidis has a magnitude of 3.68.

★ **Brightest star position** R.A. 08 43 35, Dec. −33 11 11.

Reticulum

Reticule

Also known as 'the Net', Reticulum received its current name from Nicolas-Louis de La Caille in 1752. Prior to that date, some astronomers recognized this constellation as the Rhombus.

★ **Where** Southern Hemisphere.

★ **Location** Between the constellations of Dorado and Hydrus.

★ **Best time to view** During the middle of December.

★ **Brightest star** Alpha Reticuli has a magnitude of 3.35.

★ **Brightest star position** R.A. 04 14 25, Dec. –62 28 26.

Fine lines

La Caille named this constellation to commemorate the reticule, the network of fine lines engraved at regular intervals across a telescope's eyepiece. The reticule allowed astronomers to make much more accurate estimates of the distances between stars.

349

Sagitta

Arrow

Known from the earliest times, Sagitta is a small constellation. The ancient astronomers of Greece, Persia and Rome were all agreed that this pattern of stars was an arrow in flight across the heavens.

Cupid's dart

The Arrow has gradually lost all its warlike connotations. It is now seen as the arrow fired from the bow of Cupid or Eros in order to make a person fall in love.

★ **Where** Northern and Southern hemispheres.

★ **Location** Between the constellations of Delphinus and Hercules.

★ **Best time to view** During the last week of August.

★ **Brightest star** Gamma Sagittae has a magnitude of 3.47.

★ **Brightest star position** R.A. 19 58 45, Dec. +19 29 32.

Sagittarius
Archer

Of the 12 constellations of the zodiac, Sagittarius is the most southerly. The Babylonians were the first to identify this constellation as a mounted archer. Greek astronomers preferred to interpret it as one of the centaurs.

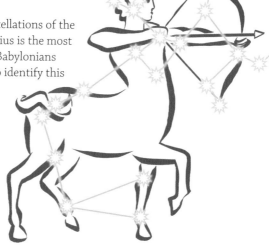

★ **Where** Southern Hemisphere.

★ **Location** Between the constellations of Capricornus and Scorpius.

★ **Best time to view** During the first week of August.

★ **Brightest star** Kaus Australis (Epsilon Sagittarii) has a magnitude of 1.85.

★ **Brightest star position** R.A. 18 24 10, Dec. −34 23 05.

Too many names

The Swan Nebula (M17), at the northern end of Sagittarius, suffers from having too many names. It is also known as the Omega Nebula, the Horseshoe Nebula, and the Check-mark Nebula.

Scorpius

Scorpion

One of the zodiacal constellations, Scorpius was originally identified and named in ancient Babylonia. Greek astronomers interpreted it as the scorpion that killed the mighty Orion with its sting.

Space butterfly

Scorpius contains several bright clusters of stars, one of which (M6) is known as the Butterfly because of its shape. Although this cluster is over 1200 light years away, it is easily viewed through binoculars.

★ **Where** Southern Hemisphere.

★ **Location** Between the constellations of Sagittarius and Norma.

★ **Best time to view** During the first week of July.

★ **Brightest star** Antares (Alpha Scorpii) has a magnitude of 0.96 and is 330 light years away.

★ **Brightest star position** R.A. 16 29 24, Dec. −26 25 55.

Sculptor

Sculptor

Originally named Apparatus Sculptoris (the Sculptor's Tools) the name of this constellation has since been shortened to the Sculptor. It is one of the 14 Southern Hemisphere constellations that were first identified by La Caille in his 1752 star atlas.

★ **Where** Southern Hemisphere.

★ **Location** Between the constellations of Cetus and Phoenix.

★ **Best time to view** During the last week of October.

★ **Brightest star** Alpha Sculptoris has a magnitude of 4.31.

★ **Brightest star position** R.A. 00 58 36, Dec. –29 21 27.

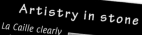

Artistry in stone

La Caille clearly intended to pay tribute to both the arts and the sciences when he named his constellations.

However, it is unclear whether he preferred sculpture (given two starry memorials) to painting (given one).

Scutum

Shield

A small constellation, Scutum was identified by Hevelius in the 17th century. He originally named it Scutum Sobiescianum (Sobieski's Shield) in honour of the Polish king John Sobieski, but other astronomers later dropped this royal association.

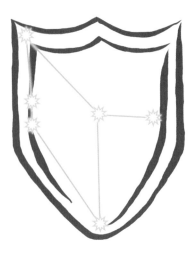

Natural beauty

Scutum contains one of the most spectacular open clusters in the night sky. Designated M11, the Wild Duck Cluster is one of the most compact of all star clusters and it presents a stunning view through a small telescope.

★ **Where** Northern and Southern hemispheres.

★ **Location** Between the constellations of Sagittarius and Serpens.

★ **Best time to view** During the first week of August.

★ **Brightest star** Alpha Scuti has a magnitude of 3.85.

★ **Brightest star position** R.A. 18 35 12, Dec. −08 14 39.

Serpens
Serpent

On Ptolemy's original list, Serpens is the only constellation that is divided into two parts. Ophiuchus (the Serpent Bearer) separates the head (Serpens Caput) from the tail (Serpens Cauda).

- ★ **Where** Northern and Southern hemispheres.
- ★ **Location** Between the constellations of Hercules and Libra.
- ★ **Best time to view** During the first week of July.
- ★ **Brightest star** Unukalhai (Alpha Serpentis) has a magnitude of 2.65 and is 88 light years away.
- ★ **Brightest star position** R.A. 15 44 16, Dec. +06 25 32.

Star birth

The Eagle Nebula (IC 4703) in the Serpent's tail is one of the places where astronomers have detected the process of star formation. Stars are being born inside swirling pillars of gas, nicknamed 'elephant trunks'.

Sextans

Sextant

Johannes Hevelius
first identified
Sextans in 1689.
He originally
named it Sextans
Urania (Astronomer's
Sextant) in order to
commemorate the loss
of his own sextant when his
observatory caught fire.

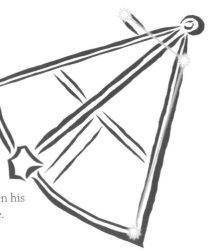

Spun stars

The Spindle Galaxy (NGC 3115) is located within the constellation of Sextans. This distant galaxy got its name because its edge-on view looks like an old-fashioned spindle used for spinning thread.

★ **Where** Northern and Southern hemispheres.

★ **Location** Between the constellations of Leo and Hydra.

★ **Best time to view** During the last week in March.

★ **Brightest star** Alpha Sextantis has a magnitude of 4.49.

★ **Brightest star position** R.A. 10 07 56, Dec. −00 22 18.

Taurus
Bull

One of the 12 constellations of the zodiac, Taurus is easily spotted. According to Greek mythology, Zeus, the king of the gods, turned himself into a beautiful white bull in order to kidnap Europa, the daughter of Cadmus.

★ **Where** Northern and Southern hemispheres.

★ **Location** Between the constellations of Orion and Aries.

★ **Best time to view** During the first week of January.

★ **Brightest star** Aldebaran (Alpha Tauri) has a magnitude of 0.85 and is 68 light years away.

★ **Brightest star position** R.A. 04 35 55, Dec. +16 30 33.

First crab

The Crab Nebula in Taurus has the designation M1. This is because it was the first of the non-stellar objects (clusters, nebulae and galaxies) to be listed by the French astronomer Charles Messier in 1771.

Telescopium

Telescope

Positioned near to Corona Australis and Sagittarius, Telescopium is one of the constellations that La Caille added to the sky as a result of his observations from South Africa. In order to produce this telescope, he had to 'borrow' stars from neighbouring constellations.

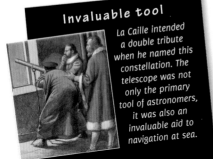

Invaluable tool

La Caille intended a double tribute when he named this constellation. The telescope was not only the primary tool of astronomers, it was also an invaluable aid to navigation at sea.

★ **Where** Southern Hemisphere.

★ **Location** Between the constellations of Indus and Ara.

★ **Best time to view** During the middle of August.

★ **Brightest star** Alpha Telescopii has a magnitude of 3.51.

★ **Brightest star position** R.A. 18 26 58, Dec. −45 58 06.

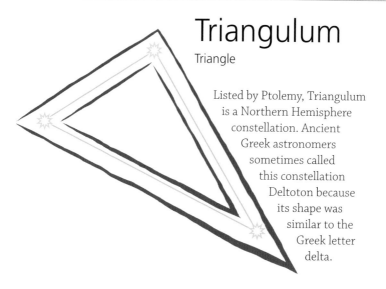

Triangulum

Triangle

Listed by Ptolemy, Triangulum is a Northern Hemisphere constellation. Ancient Greek astronomers sometimes called this constellation Deltoton because its shape was similar to the Greek letter delta.

★ **Where** Northern and Southern hemispheres.

★ **Location** Between the constellations of Aries and Andromeda.

★ **Best time to view** During the last week of November.

★ **Brightest star** Beta Trianguli has a magnitude of 3.0.

★ **Brightest star position** R.A. 02 09 32, Dec. +34 59 14.

Cosmic pinwheel

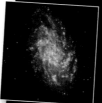

Located at the edge of Triangulum is a spiral galaxy (M33), which is sometimes called the Pinwheel Galaxy. From Earth we see this galaxy face-on. A telescope with a wide angle of view is necessary to appreciate its full glory.

Triangulum Australe

Southern Triangle

Introduced at the beginning of the
17th century, Triangulum Australe
is an easily identified triangle
of bright stars. It was
deliberately named to be
a southern counterpart
to the constellation
of Triangulum in
the Northern
Hemisphere.

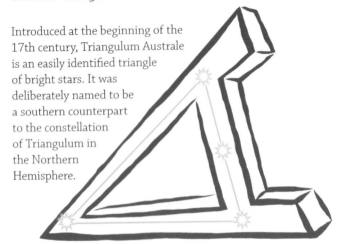

Drawing instrument

Although it was a southern
counterpart, the name
of this constellation is
significant. It is located
next to Norma and
Circinus, which
represent
other drawing
instruments
used by carpenters
and builders.

★ **Where** Southern Hemisphere.

★ **Location** Between the
constellations of Pavo
and Circinus.

★ **Best time to view** During the
last week of June.

★ **Brightest star** Atria (Alpha
Trianguli Australis) has a
magnitude of 1.92 and is
55 light years away.

★ **Brightest star position**
R.A. 16 48 40, Dec. –69 01 39.

Tucana
Toucan

In 1603, German astronomer Johann Bayer published his star atlas. Tucana is one of the Southern Bird constellations that were identified for the first time in this book.

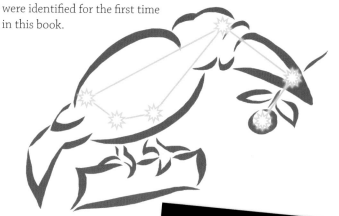

★ **Where** Southern Hemisphere.

★ **Location** Between the constellations of Eridanus and Pavo.

★ **Best time to view** During the last week of October.

★ **Brightest star** Alpha Tucanae has a magnitude of 2.86.

★ **Brightest star position** R.A. 22 18 30, Dec. –60 15 3.5

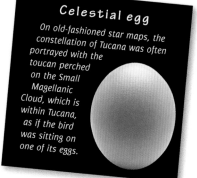

Celestial egg
On old-fashioned star maps, the constellation of Tucana was often portrayed with the toucan perched on the Small Magellanic Cloud, which is within Tucana, as if the bird was sitting on one of its eggs.

Ursa Major

Great Bear

Well known, Ursa Major is one of Ptolemy's constellations. According to Greek mythology, the larger of the two starry bears represents the woman Callisto who was turned into a bear by the goddess Hera.

Eyes in the sky

The unaided eye cannot see the Owl Nebula (M97) in Ursa Major. A small telescope shows only a dim oval shape, but a larger telescope reveals that this planetary nebula contains two stars that form the owl's eyes.

★ **Where** Northern Hemisphere.

★ **Location** Between the constellations of Canes Venatici and Lynx.

★ **Best time to view** During the last week of April.

★ **Brightest star** Alioth (Epsilon Ursae Majoris) has a magnitude of 1.77.

★ **Brightest star position** R.A. 12 54 02, Dec. +55 37 55.

Ursa Minor

Little Bear

In about 600 BC, Ursa Minor received its name from the Greek astronomer Thales. He named it to represent Callisto's son Arcas who was also turned into a bear before being placed in the heavens.

★ **Where** Northern Hemisphere.

★ **Location** Between the constellations of Cepheus and Draco.

★ **Best time to view** During the middle of June.

★ **Brightest star** Polaris (Alpha Ursae Minoris) has a magnitude of 1.99, and is 680 light years away.

★ **Brightest star position** R.A. 02 31 50, Dec. +89 15 5.1

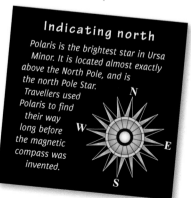

Indicating north

Polaris is the brightest star in Ursa Minor. It is located almost exactly above the North Pole, and is the north Pole Star. Travellers used Polaris to find their way long before the magnetic compass was invented.

Vela

Sail

Once a part of a large constellation named Argo, Vela represents a sail. Ptolemy invented Argo to commemorate the ship that carried the hero Jason on his mythical quest for the Golden Fleece. Argo was later split up into three separate constellations.

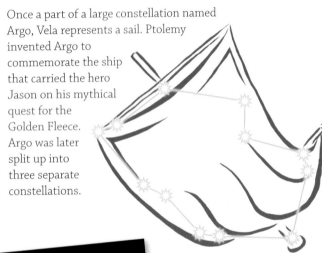

False cross

Vela contains a group of faint stars that form a very similar shape to the famous Crux Australis (Southern Cross). For this reason, these stars are sometimes referred to as the 'False Cross'.

★ **Where** Southern Hemisphere.

★ **Location** Between the constellations of Antlia and Carina.

★ **Best time to view** During the middle of March.

★ **Brightest star** Regor (Gamma Velorum) has a magnitude of 1.78.

★ **Brightest star position** R.A. 08 09 32, Dec. −47 20 12.

Virgo

Maiden

According to Greek mythology, Virgo was associated with both the goddess Artemis and the incorruptible spirit of justice. Virgo is the biggest of the 12 constellations of the zodiac.

- ★ **Where** Northern and Southern hemispheres.
- ★ **Location** Between the constellations of Libra and Leo.
- ★ **Best time to view** During the middle of May.
- ★ **Brightest star** Spica (Alpha Virginis) has a magnitude of 0.98 and is 257 light years away.
- ★ **Brightest star position** R.A. 13 25 11, Dec. −11 09 41.

Hatband

The Sombrero Galaxy (M104), which is located at the southern edge of Virgo, got its name because it looks like a wide-brimmed Mexican hat. A 'hatband' of dust stretching across the galaxy heightens the resemblance.

Volans

Flying Fish

European explorers encountered many exotic creatures for the first time while voyaging the Indian and Pacific oceans. Volans was named to commemorate the flying fish.

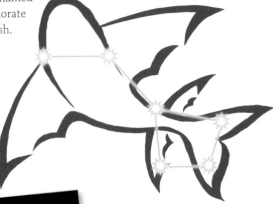

Winged fish

None of the creatures encountered in tropical waters by European explorers caused as much amazement as flying fish. These fish cannot really fly, but they can glide for dozens of metres and often landed on ship's decks.

★ **Where** Southern Hemisphere.

★ **Location** Between the constellations of Carina and Mensa.

★ **Best time to view** During the last week of February.

★ **Brightest star** Gamma Volantis is a double star with magnitudes of 4.0 and 5.9.

★ **Brightest star position** R.A. 07 08 42, Dec. –70 29 50.

Vulpecula

Fox

In 1687, Vulpecula was named by Hevelius. He originally named this constellation Vulpecula cum Anser (the Fox with the Goose) but only the fox remains, the goose has long since been forgotten.

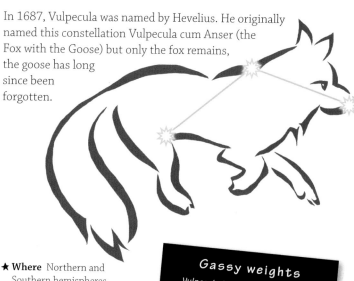

★ **Where** Northern and Southern hemispheres.

★ **Location** Between the constellations of Cygnus and Sagitta.

★ **Best time to view** During the last week of August.

★ **Brightest star** Alpha Vulpeculae has a magnitude of 4.44.

★ **Brightest star position** R.A. 19 28 42, Dec. +24 39 24.

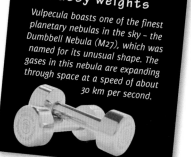

Gassy weights

Vulpecula boasts one of the finest planetary nebulas in the sky – the Dumbbell Nebula (M27), which was named for its unusual shape. The gases in this nebula are expanding through space at a speed of about 30 km per second.

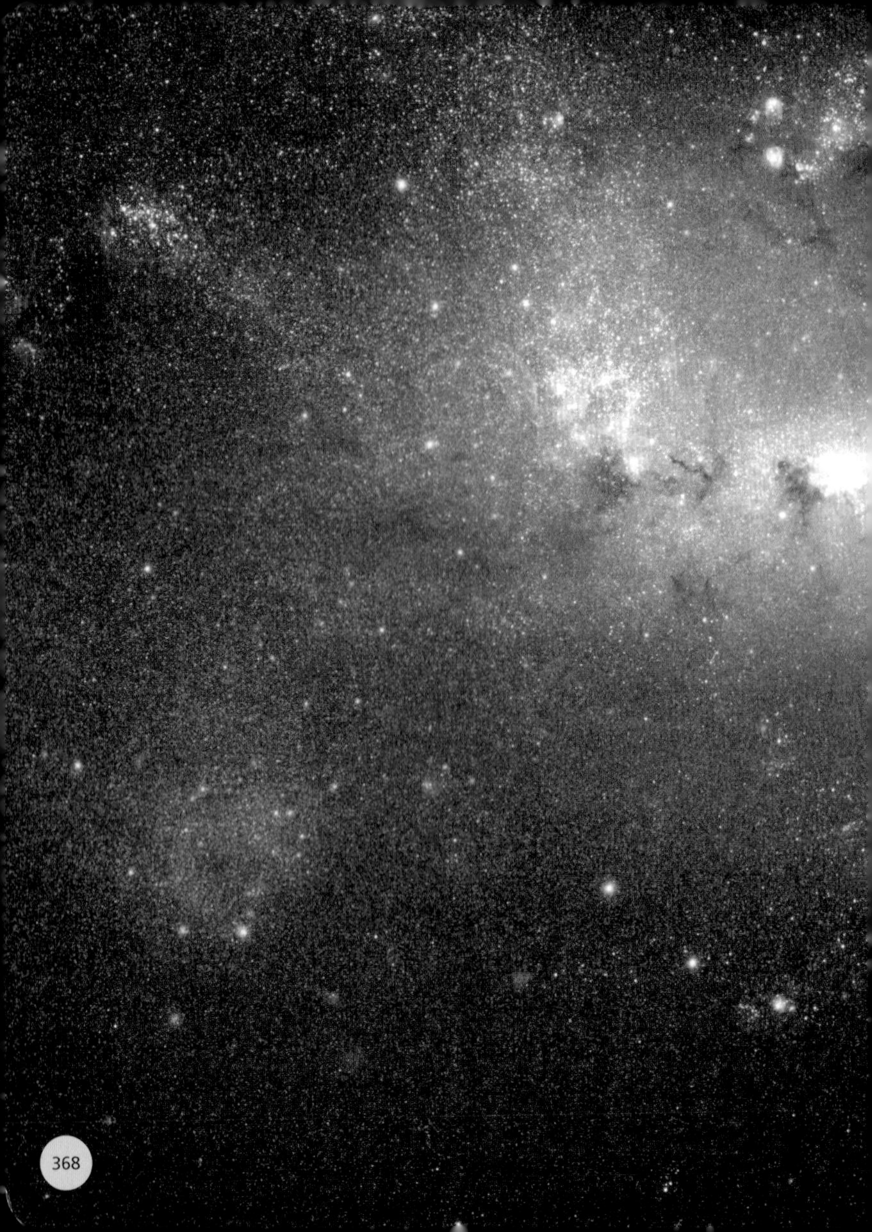

Index

Index

Entries in **bold** refer
to main subject entries;
entries in *italics* refer
to illustrations.